THE BRITIS
HORSE SOCIE

CW00539659

HUMBERSIDE ON HORSEBACK

AVAILABLE IN THIS SERIES

The Cotswolds on Horseback
Wiltshire on Horseback
Westmorland on Horseback
The Ridgeway Downs on Horseback
Exmoor on Horseback
Somerset on Horseback
Hampshire on Horseback
Leicestershire & Rutland on Horseback
Humberside on Horseback

First published 1995
by The British Horse Society
Access & Rights of Way Department
British Equestrian Centre
Stoneleigh Park, Kenilworth
Warwickshire CV8 2LR

A catalogue record for this book is available from the British Library

ISBN 1 899016 06 6

Printed by:
Tripod Press Limited, 7 Wise Street, Leamington Spa, CV31 3AP

Distribution: The British Horse Society, Stoneleigh Park, Kenilworth, Warwickshire, CV8 2LR

CONTENTS

Page No

Acknowledgements   4

Foreword   5

Introduction   6

An Introduction to Humberside   9

The Humberside Network   14

TRAILS

1.	Burton upon Stather - 15 miles	18
2.	Crowle - 15 miles	20
3.	Huggate - 25 miles	23
4.	Great Givendale - 13 miles	28
5.	Millington Ride - 21 miles	30
6.	Garton on the Wolds - 14 miles	34
7.	Saltmarshe - 15 miles	36
8.	Wold Newton - South Humberside - 15 miles	38
9.	Hornsea - 13 miles	42
10.	Rudston - 15 miles	44
11.	Burton Pidsea - 13 miles	46
12.	Adlingfleet - 16 miles	48
13.	Brantingham - 19 miles	50
14.	Kiplingcoates - 11 miles	52
15.	Around Bishop Burton Wold - 11 miles	54
16.	Around Goodmanham Wold - 20 or 25 miles	57
17.	Holderness - Halsham - 17 miles	60
18.	Bishop Wilton - 9 miles	64
19.	Barton upon Humber - 15 miles	66
20.	Melton Ross - 15 miles	68
21.	Barnetby - 15 miles	70
22.	Seaton Ross - 18 miles	72
23.	Newport - 11 miles	74
24.	Leven - 20 miles	76
25.	Bubwith to Londesborough - 15 miles	78
26.	Londesborough to Tickton - 15 miles	82
27.	North Cave - 15 miles	85
28.	Hive - 15 miles	88
29.	Withernwick - 11 miles	90

ACKNOWLEDGEMENTS

A number of people and organisations have given their time and expertise to provide details for this book or contributed in some other way.

In particular the British Horse Society would like to thank Val Armstrong who assisted in developing and surveying routes, Eric Jones for his cover photograph, Kirsten Alford for the many line drawings and Humberside County Council for their generous financial support.

But above all, the Society would wish to pay tribute to Hazel Wink their tireless, talented and dedicated County Bridleways Officer, who masterminded the entire initiative and carried out the major part of the work, with assistance from Andrew Armstrong.

FOREWORD

When the British Horse Society launched its ARROW Project in 1991, few people could have foreseen the tremendous response and commitment that it would provoke from recreational drivers and riders. That eight trail guide books were in print by May 1994 with the prospect of a further eight in 1995, is testament to their dedication and talent. I am delighted, on behalf of all equestrians, to pay tribute to those who have made such a unique contribution towards the achievement of a network of circular and linear trails.

The Society is concerned that little had been achieved for carriage drivers within ARROW: however it is pleasing that some progress has now been made and that a number of driving trails will be featured this year and in subsequent years.

It is a fact that drivers are restricted to Byways and Unclassified County Roads, thus there are fewer chances to provide them with off-road driving opportunities. This calls for a separate approach, with our Rights of Way staff and volunteers working hand-in-glove with drivers and driving organisations, in order to identify and claim lost routes. The Access & Rights of Way Policy Committee, in overseeing this initiative, will do all in its power to gain maximum benefit for drivers from this important partnership.

As it is virtually impossible to produce a circular or linear route without incorporating some metalled highways it is difficult to lay claim to having opened up a given mileage of 'off-road' riding.

What can be claimed however, is that by the end of 1995 details of up to 350 trails, totalling about 5000 miles, should be in print.

With a further eight books planned for 1996/97 and others in prospect towards the millennium, the Society can, with some justification, feel proud to have contributed to the safety and the greater enjoyment of those who take pleasure from riding and carriage driving.

E A T BONNOR-MAURICE
Chairman, British Horse Society

January 1995

INTRODUCTION

The British Horse Society's ARROW Project aims to identify open and usable routes of varying length and shape (circular, figure-of-eight or linear) to help riders and carriage drivers to enjoy the countryside by means, as far as possible, of the network of public rights of way and the minor vehicular highways. This collection of rides is the result of research and mapping by volunteers who took up the challenge of the ARROW initiative with such enthusiasm and effort.

I am faced with the equally daunting challenge of writing an introductory chapter. Should I write reams about each topic or try simply to point you in the right direction? I have decided upon the second method as the search for information is itself highly educative and stays in the mind better than reading it all in one place. Also, since we all have different expectations of our holiday, a very full guide seemed wrong. Nevertheless, there are a few pointers I would like to suggest to you.

The most important one is to start your planning several months in advance of the trip, including a visit to the area you intend to ride in. You should make endless lists of things to DO (e.g. get the saddle checked) and things to CHECK OUT (can you read a map, for instance). You may find joining the local BHS Endurance Riding Group very helpful, as there you will meet people who can give you information about the degree of fitness needed for yourself and your horse (feeding for fitness not dottiness) , and many other useful hints on adventurous riding. You may also enjoy some of the Pleasure rides organised by the group or by the local Riding Club. These are usually about 15-20 miles and you ride in company, though using

a map. You may find them under the title Training Rides. These rides will get both of you used to going into strange country. If you usually ride on well-known tracks, then your horse will find it nerve-racking to go off into new territory, and you yourself may also find the excitement of deep country a bit surprising, so try to widen your experience at home before you go off on holiday.

ACCOMMODATION

Decide how far you wish to ride each day of your holiday, book overnight accommodation for both of you and if possible visit it to see if the five-star suite on offer to your horse is what he is used to. Decide if you want to stable him or to turn him out at the end of the day, and arrange to drop off some food for him, as he will not relish hard work on a diet of green grass, nor will he enjoy a change in his usual food. If you are to have a back-up vehicle, of course, then you will not need to do some of this, but you should certainly make a preliminary visit if you can. The BHS publish a Bed & Breakfast Guide for Horses which is a list of people willing to accommodate horses, and sometimes riders, overnight. The Society does not inspect these places, so you should check everything in advance.

FITNESS

You and your horse should be fit. For both of you , this is a process taking about two months. If you and/or your horse are not in the full flush of youth, then it may take a bit longer. The office chair, the factory floor, or the household duties do not make or keep you fit, but carefully planned exercise will. Remember that no matter how fit your horse seems, he does not keep himself fit - you get him fit. There are several books with details of fitness programmes for a series of rides. Do not forget to build in a rest day during your holiday - neither of you can keep going all the time, day after day. Miles of walking may get you fit, but it uses different muscles from riding; you may get a surprise when you start riding longer distances. It seems to me that the further you intend to ride, the longer your preparation should be. Nothing can be done in a hurry.

Your horse should be obedient, so work on that. If you want him to stand, then he must stand. If you want to go through water, then he must be prepared to walk down a slope or even step down off a bank to go through the stream, so start with puddles and insist that he go through the middle. Does he help you open gates? I hope so, or you will have a great deal of mounting and dismounting to do. Does he tie up - this is essential if you are to have a peaceful pint at lunchtime.

MAPS

Can you read a map? Can you make and read a grid reference (usually referred to as GR)? Get a Pathfinder map of your area and take yourself for a walk and see if you end up where you expect to. Learn to know exactly where you are on the map, and how to understand the symbols (if your map shows hilly ground, the journey will take longer). Can you work out how long a ride is in miles and roughly how long it will take? You will be using rights of way and it is very important that you stay in the line of the path - that is the only place you have a right to be, and you may deviate from that line only as much as is necessary to get you round an obstruction on the path. You are going to be riding over land that forms

part of someone's work place and that fact must be respected. It is only by the efforts of farmers and landowners that the countryside exists in its present form - so that we may enjoy it as we pass by.

You will need to know the grid reference (GR.) of the start and end of the various tracks you are to use. Get a copy of an Ordnance Survey (OS) Landranger map and really learn the details on the right-hand side, some of which explain how to arrive at a Grid Reference. Learn to go in the door (Eastings - from left to right) and up the stairs (Northings - from bottom to top). There is a great deal of information on the Landranger maps and not so much on the Pathfinders, but the Pathfinder gives more details on the map itself, so that is the map you will use for the actual ride. Or you may care to buy a Landranger of the area you are visiting and, using a highlighter pen, mark in all the rides you want to make, so that you can see through the marks you make. Then get from any Outdoor shop a map case which will allow you to read the map without taking it out of the case and which you can secure round yourself. Also, you should know if you are facing north, south, east or west as you ride. Quite important if you think about it, as it is no good riding into the sunset if you are meant to be going south. Plastic orienteering compasses are cheap and reliable.

TACK

Have your tack thoroughly checked by your saddler, as there is nothing so annoying as a sore back which could have been prevented, or an unnecessarily broken girth strap. How are you going to carry the essential headcollar and rope each day? What about spare shoes, or a false shoe?

What to take on the ride depends on how

much back-up you have. If you have to carry a change of clothes, etc., then you are into very careful planning indeed - balance saddle bag, the lot. If you are based at your first night stop all the time, then life is much easier. You should always carry a first aid kit for horse and rider. You will also have to plan how to wash the girth and numnah. Remember our delightful climate and always carry a waterproof and additional warm clothing - it never pays to gamble with rain and wind.

SAFETY

It is always wiser to ride in company. The other person can always hold your horse, or pull you out of the ditch, as well as being someone to talk to about the excitements of the day and to help plan everything. You should always wear a BSI riding hat, properly secured, and also safe footwear. You need a clearly defined heel and a smooth sole. Even if riding in company, tell someone where you are going and roughly how long you expect to take. If affordable, take a portable telephone. Make a list of the things you must carry every day and check it before leaving base.

INSURANCE

You should have Third Party Legal Liability Insurance. This will protect you if you or your horse cause a bit of mayhem (accidentally!). Membership of the BHS gives you this type of insurance, plus Personal Accident Insurance as part of the membership package. Check your household insurance to make sure it covers riding before you rely only on that, as some insurances do not. You should always have this type of cover when venturing forth into the outside world, even if it is an hours hack from home.

PARKING

If you intend to box to the start of the day's ride, either have someone to take the box away or make sure it is safely, securely and considerately parked. If you have to make arrangements to park, do it well in advance or the contact may well have gone to market or the hairdressers when you make a last minute call. Have the vehicle number etched on to the windows for security.

MONEY

This is vital, so work out a system of getting money if necessary. Sadly we can no longer gallop up to the bank and lead Dobbin into the cashier's queue, nor do most banks have hitching rails. Post Offices are more numerous and might be a useful alternative. Always have the price of a telephone call on you.

Lastly, if you do run into problems of blocked paths or boggy ones, write to the Highway Authority of the relevant county council and tell them. Then you can do something about it. You might even think of adopting a path near home and keeping an eye on it, telling your own county council of any difficulties you encounter. It is through such voluntary work that these rides have been made possible.

Wherever you ride, always do it responsibly, with care of the land, consideration for the farmer and courtesy for all other users. Remember the Country Code and enjoy your ARROW Riding.

I hope this chapter will have started you planning and making lists. If I seem to be always writing about forward planning it is only because I usually leave things to the last minute, which causes chaos!

PHILIPPA LUARD

AN INTRODUCTION TO HUMBERSIDE

Humberside was formed in 1974 and may be still relatively unknown. It comprises the majority of the East Riding of Yorkshire, a large part of North Lincolnshire and a bit of West Yorkshire, all historic and well known areas and all still containing their own history, heritage and ways of life.

The county is one of contrasts, and wherever you ride, you will find the landscape, villages and people are all slightly different, but always interesting.

The rides to the south of the River Humber, a river that drains one-fifth of England, are on the northern Lincolnshire Wolds, a delightful range of hills containing pretty villages and unspoilt countryside. The area to the north and west is known as Glanford and some fine views are obtained across the River Trent to the flat area of the Isle of Axholme and beyond. Glanford's name was recorded in 1235 in a Charter confirming Henry III's Grant for a market to be held at Glanford Bridge, a town later to become known as Brigg. Brigg and Barton are the two towns in the area and always busy on market days. There are also two interesting country parks at Elsham Hall and Normanby Hall which are worth a visit. The countryside is not spectacular, but pleasing, maintaining its traditional rural occupations just as it has done for hundreds of years.

To the west of the River Trent is the Isle of Axholme, a vast area of land which was mainly swamps and marshes until drained by the dutchman Vermuyden 400 years ago. It contains some attractive little villages including Epworth where John and Charles Wesley were born. Today it attracts Methodists from all over the world. Another feature of the Isle is that it still retains its medieval method of strip farming, once the way all land was farmed all over England.

In medieval times the parish was divided into three or four massive 'fields' and people had a number of strips in each field. During the Enclosure Awards of the 18th century, the people were awarded blocks of land away from the village commensurate with the number of strips they had before. This led to farms being built away from the village centre and the creation of the modern day field system which exists today. Many new roads were also created, some at a width of 60 feet. They are still there today and the wide grass verges are ideal for riding on.

The area just south of the Ouse is known as Marshlands and is a quiet and peaceful area possibly best known for the RSPB site at Blacktoft Sands. Although remote, the church at Adlingfleet was recorded in the Domesday Book as having the third richest living in the country.

On the north bank are the Yorkshire Wolds, England's most northerly range of chalk hills. They are of the type found in Hardy's Wessex, the Downs of Kent and the Chilterns but nowhere are they so perfectly preserved as on the Yorkshire

Wolds. You can ride along long secluded dales or the airy tops with magnificent views all around. You will find large estates with impressive halls and parkland where the local Lord still owns vast tracts of land, a few villages and even the odd pub! It is delightful to explore, and like many other places, your only company will be sheep and skylarks. The joy of the Wolds is the peace of it all. 'Pay and Display' car parks and villages with double yellow lines have yet to reach here, and long may it remain so.

West of the Wolds stands the Vale of York, a typical English landscape of farms and villages and a colourful patchwork of crops of all descriptions.

East of the Wolds stands Holderness, Winifred Holtby's 'South Riding'. She describes it as 'the plain rising and dimpling in gentle undulations as though a giant potter had pressed his thumbs now more lightly, now more heavily, on the yet malleable clay of the spinning globe'. Its quiet villages and winding country lanes purvey peace and tranquillity. It is also noted for its churches, including the impressive one at Hedon, and the one at Patrington which is a cathedral in miniature. It includes England's most changeable piece of land at Spurn Point which is the fastest eroding coastline in Europe at the average rate of 4 metres per year! When William the Conqueror landed at Hastings in 1066, the cliff top at Withernsea was a mile further out to sea!

Further north is bustling Bridlington and the spectacular coastline of Flamborough Head dotted with coves and inlets. This is 'seabird city' with puffins, kittywakes and even the mighty gannets.

The major town on the north bank is Kingston-upon-Hull, rich in maritime history and where the old docks reach into the city centre. Beverley is the county town and well worth a visit. It is a charming market town dominated by Beverley Minster one of Europe's finest examples of Gothic architecture and a building much larger than many of England's Abbeys and Cathedrals.

All over the county you will find a rich and interesting heritage. Neolithic man was here, and a 48 feet long Longboat was found at Brigg. On the north bank at Ferriby Europe's oldest 'Plank' boat was excavated in 1946 and carbon dating put it as late Bronze Age.

The fierce Celtic tribe of the Brigantes were in the area before being overrun by the Romans on their advance northwards. They settled and built a road, Ermin Street, from Lincoln to York. Along it some fine villas were built and some of the mosaics excavated can now be seen in a Hull museum, along with many other finds. The Roman road crossed the Humber at Brough, the Roman town of Petuaria. With the withdrawal of the Roman garrisons from Britain in the 5th century, the local people sought protection and Germanic mercenaries were employed. The two tribes that came were the Angles and the Saxons. Several large Anglian cremation cemeteries have been found in various areas of the county including some of up to 600 people. Early Anglo-Saxon settlements can be identified by names ending in 'ing' or 'ingham', whilst later settlements end with 'ton', meaning enclosure or homestead - Bridlington was the homestead of Brettle.

The first Viking invaders were friendly and settled easily in the area. Their settlements end in 'by' or 'thorpe' - Grimsby was founded by the Viking Grim. There was soon, however, conflict between the English and the Danes which resulted in the battle of Brunnahburge near Barrow in AD 837 where the Danes were defeated by King Atherlston. Athelred II came to the throne and the Viking attacks were renewed. This time they came as raiders and were finally defeated at Stamford Bridge by King Harold in September 1066. Although 500 ships sailed up the Humber and Ouse, 20 ships were sufficient to take the survivors home. Much of the area was awarded to Norman knights, who had helped William the Conqueror, and several castles were built.

In the more peaceful medieval times, villages grew and prospered yet many 'died'. Today, the area has many deserted medieval villages and you can ride along sunken trackways surrounded by grassy bumps which were once the site of a thriving little community. It is an eerie feeling. Later the land was enclosed and the field system of today laid out, one which is still relatively unchanged today. The tiny Wolds farms stand protected in their three sided shelter belts, whilst many a village still has farms mixed in with cottages along the main street. Forty miles of disused railway lines are a reminder of the contribution of Victorian man, and the stupidity of the 1960's man. Yet they are owned by the council and today are important recreational routes as well as 'wildlife corridors'. You can ride between the platforms of the tiny, but once busy, rural stations. Wild flowers grow where once whistles blew and the sound of the birds replaces the sound of steam. The platforms of the once well tended stations have become overgrown and although it can be a sorry sight, it is a peaceful, safe haven for all manner of insects and butterflies and for you on your horse.

Unexploited, unexplored and unhurried are three words that best sum up the county. Rural England still exists here and hardly a 'pay and display' car park or double yellow line is in sight. The cottages are not holiday homes and the village pub is still the village pub where tractors can outnumber XR3i's!

Humberside is part old Lincolnshire and part old East Yorkshire and woe betide you if you address locals as Humbersiders! 'Yellow-belly Yorkie Pride' still exists, as do local characters, customs and cultures.

It is a rich mix of landscapes and places. All the rides are through different areas and we hope you will enjoy discovering this very pleasant part of rural England for yourself. You will find a warm welcome, even from the old die-hard farmer who will wonder why you want to ride along the bridleways and byways that arose for a functional purpose of times long past. That is the joy of a rights of way network, to ride along routes whose history is shrouded in the mists of time. Are you riding on a road the Romans used, or an old medieval trackway? Maybe you are on a route used by farmers long ago to take their goods to market, or along a Victorian railway line. You may even be riding across a World War II airfield.

You can even ride along the route of England's oldest horse race, the Kiplingcotes Derby. First run in 1519 as a test for horses after the long winter lay-off, it has been run every year without fail since. The person that comes second normally gets more than the person that comes first!! Can you find out why?

So, come and ride the Wolds, we have got two areas for you. Discover the Isle of Axholme and Holderness, both very contrasting areas but enjoyable. Ride through the Vale of York and attractive Glanford. Humberside is a county of old historical counties, contrasts and cultures all in one. It is a peaceful and relaxing area and those that have discovered it have found it a surprise and a delight. Coast and countryside are here to be explored.

Many of the rides are also suitable for winter rides, the area having a low rainfall and the Wolds being chalk, are soon safe to ride. The area, being agricultural changes through the seasons and a ride in autumn after the crops have been harvested is totally different from a ride in the spring. It is a working landscape that can be interesting for there is always something happening around you, unlike some areas that stay the same throughout the year.

Don't look for tourists for you will be the tourist in many areas, on your own and at peace with the joys of the countryside.

As always, stop and stare, look and listen. Take your time and enjoy your visit

We look forward to welcoming you.

IAN INGLES
SENIOR RIGHTS OF WAY OFFICER
HUMBERSIDE COUNTY COUNCIL

CODE FOR RIDING & DRIVING RESPONSIBLY

THE BRITISH HORSE SOCIETY

1. **Riders and carriage drivers** everywhere should proceed with courtesy, care and consideration. The British Horse Society recommends the following:

    Care for the Land
    Do not stray off the line of the path;
    Do not damage timber or hedgerows by jumping;
    Remember that horses' hooves can damage surfaces in bad weather;
    Pay particular attention to protected areas that have significant historical and/or biological value, as they are extremely sensitive to damage.

    Courtesy to other users
    Remember that walkers, cyclists and other riders may be elderly, disabled, children or simply frightened of horses; whenever possible acknowledge courtesy shown by drivers of motor vehicles.

    Consideration for the farmer
    Shut the gate behind you;
    Ride slowly past all stock;
    Do not ride on cultivated land unless the right of way crosses it;
    Dogs are seldom welcome on farmland or moorland unless on a lead or under close control.

2. **Observe local byelaws**

3. **Ride or drive with care on the roads** and take the BHS Riding and Road Safety Test. Always make sure that you can be seen at night or in bad visibility, by wearing the right kind of reflective/fluorescent aids.

4. **Groups from riding establishments** should contain reasonable numbers, for reasons of both safety and amenity. They should never exceed twenty in total **including** the relevant number of escorts as indicated in BHS guidelines on levels of capability among riders in groups, available on request. Rides should not deviate from the right of way or permitted route and regard must be shown at all times for growing crops, shutting and securing of gates and the consideration and courtesy due to others.

5. **Always obey the Country Code in every way possible:**
    Enjoy the countryside and respect its life and work
    Guard against all risk of fire
    Fasten all gates
    Keep your dogs under close control
    Keep to public paths across farmland
    Use gates and stiles to cross fences, hedges and walls
    Leave livestock, crops and machinery alone
    Take your litter home
    Help keep all water clean
    Protect wildlife, plants and trees
    Take special care on country roads
    Make no unnecessary noise.

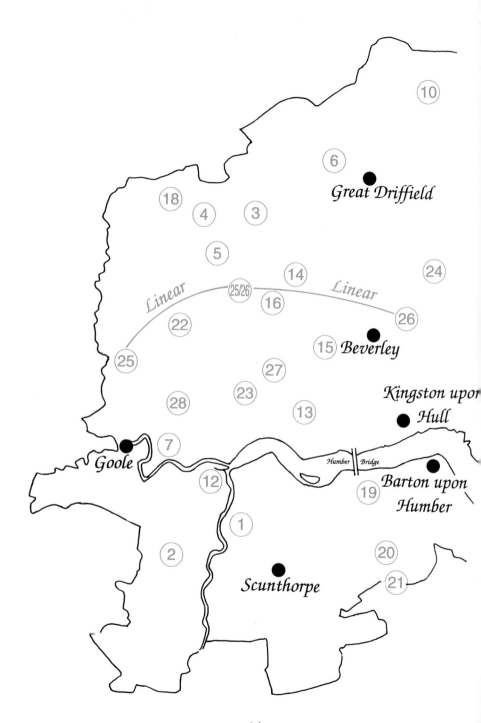

Great Driffield

Beverley

Kingston upon Hull

Goole

Humber Bridge

Barton upon Humber

Scunthorpe

Linear

Linear

HUMBERSIDE
ON HORSEBACK

Bridlington

North Sea

Hornsea

(9)

(29)

(11)

Withernsea

(17)

River Humber

Grimsby

(8)

Cleethorpes

PARK AND RIDE

In the increasing climate of theft, we have started a scheme called 'Park & Ride' Rather than use public roads and car parks, provided you contact them in advance and your requested date is convenient to them, any of the people listed below are prepared to offer private parking facilities. There will be a small fee for this facility This does not mean that somebody will 'baby-sit' your vehicle, nor does it mean you will have any re-course in law should the vehicle be stolen, or damaged, whilst on their property. However, we do feel that it gives a bit more peace of mind than leaving your vehicle in open places or isolated areas.

Mr & Mrs Keyes, Eastgate Cottage, Woldgate, Kilham(10)	01262 420358
Mrs J Elliott, East Riding Equestrian Centre, Stoney Carr Farm, Newport (23 & 28)	01430 440835
Mr & Mrs Wilson, Robeanne Farmhouse, Shiptonthorpe (16)	01430 873312
Mr & Mrs Dickinson, Aughton Hall, Aughton (25)	01757 289046
Mr & Mrs Prince, Warren Farm, Warter (3 & 5)	01759 304091
Mrs Abu Hamdan, High Belthorpe, Bishop Wilton (4 & 18)	01759 368238
Mrs Sweeting, Dairy Farm, Saltmarshe (7)	01430 430677
Mrs Southwell, Arram Hall, Seaton, Hornsea (9)	01964 533739
Mr & Mrs Cammidge, Northern Shire Horse Centre, North Newbald (15 & 16)	01430 827480
Mr & Mrs Travis, Elmtree Tack Shop, Halsham (17)	01964 612391
Mr R Lewis, Manor Farm, Burton Pidsea (11)	01964 670463
Mr & Mrs Winlow, Seaton Old Hall Farm, Seaton Ross (22)	01759 318469
Thornes Motor Services, Derwent Garage, Bubwith (25)	01757 288378
Mrs Hart, Crow Tree Farm, Arram (26)	01964 550167

SAFETY

Know your Highway Code (1994 Edition)

In Particular Paragraphs 216/224

RIDE WITH:

CARE

- For the Land

COURTESY

- To other users

CONSIDERATION

- For the Farmer

Disclaimer

Whilst all due care was taken in the preparation of these maps neither the British Horse Society nor their agents or servants accept any responsibility for any inaccuracies which may occur. It should be borne in mind that landmarks and conditions change and it is assumed that the user has a Pathfinder or Landranger Ordnance Survey map and a compass.

The Country Code should be observed by every rider, with great care being taken to keep to the line of the Public Rights of Way particularly when crossing farmland.

BURTON UPON STATHER

A 15 MILE CIRCULAR TRAIL (CLOCKWISE)

Ordnance Survey Map:
Landranger: 112

Parking & Starting Point:
Parking is available for three cars with trailers, in a lay-by on the Flixborough Industrial Estate. The Industrial Estate is approached from Flixborough Stather and is by a high wire fence. (GR.867145). This is also your starting point.

Note:
UCR - Unclassified County Road

Of Interest:
Burton upon Stather was once a busy market town. You will notice the interesting old buildings and shop fronts. The original church was Norman and contains several monuments to the Sheffield family, who were once the Dukes of Buckingham. At the bottom of the hill in Burton upon Stather you will see the wharf, which is still quite busy, where Cargo ships frequently load and unload their cargo. By the Ferry House Public House, you can see the landing stages of the ferry which used to operate over the Trent to Garthorpe. As you turn left along The Cliff (GR.009107) you will see the finest views of the River Trent and the Isle of Axholme.

Julian's Bower, one of the few remaining turf mazes in the country is also along

this route. It is believed to have been created by monks from a nearby monastic establishment, and from it you can see the splendid views of the confluence of the Rivers Trent and Ouse, which form the River Humber. The lighthouse at Trent Falls marks the exact spot. To the north the views are of the Yorkshire Wolds.

Route Description:

From your parking place head north north-west, turning left off the main Flixborough road and take the UCR under the disused railway and follow to the bridleway at Burton Wood. Ride along the edge of the wood, climbing steadily. *Here you can enjoy the excellent views to the west across the River Trent and Luddington village.*

Climb steeply uphill into Burton upon Stather. Take the first turning left and turn left again along the main street to go left down the hill in front of the church (GR.870178).

At the bottom of the hill is the wharf. Take the bridlepath on the right and follow the well defined path up the hill to turn left along The Cliff (GR.869187) and ride towards Julian's Bower (GR.880218).

Along this path is Kell Well which is said to have curious properties, but nobody seems to know just what these are.

Just before Julian's Bower, you will see

18

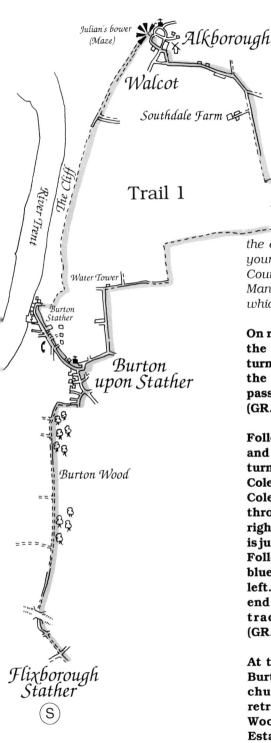

Trail 1

the earthworks of Countess Close on your left. These are named after Countess Lucy, who owned Walcot Manor during the Norman period and which lies on your right,

On reaching Julian's Bower, go from the maze and through the gate to turn right along the road. On meeting the crossroads, go straight across, passing an old windmill on your left (GR.883216).

Follow the road for about 0.50 miles and at a left-hand bend in the road, turn right along the bridleway to Coleby (GR.892210). When you reach Coleby, turn right along the road through the hamlet and then go right on to another bridleway which is just after Coleby Hall (GR.899195). Follow the headland and look for the blue way marker telling you to turn left. Follow this marker and at the end of this field turn right along the track past the water tower (GR.875188).

At the road turn left and return to Burton upon Stather, passing the church and going uphill and so retrace your route back along Burton Woods to Flixborough Industrial Estate and your parking place.

19

CROWLE

A 17 MILE CIRCULAR TRAIL (ANTI-CLOCKWISE)

Ordnance Survey Map:
Landranger: 112

Parking & Starting Point:
Parking is available at the north end of Wharf Road, Ealand, either on the hard standing area or on the grass verge (GR.782117). This is also your starting point.

Note:
1. UCR - Unclassified County Road
2. Your attention is drawn to the fact that this route crosses a dual carriageway. It is regularly used by horse riders but it is important that you are aware of this point.

Of Interest:

Crowle Moors is an important conservation area and attracts many varieties of butterfly during the summer. In hot weather watch out for adders basking on the sandy paths. The road taking you away from the A18 is teeming with wild life. Watch out for water birds - herons fish the river bank and there are lots of swans and moorhens. If you are very quiet you may see stoats playing in the grass. In the spring the river banks are covered in daffodils, bluebells and primroses.

Route Description:

From your parking place, ride east along Ealand Outgate and take the first turning on the right along Main Street. Ride along the road and look for and turn left along the bridleway (Bonnyhald Road).*After about 0.5 miles you will see Railway House which stands at the side of the disused Axholme Joint Railway. An arched viaduct used to carry the line across the canal, main railway line and drainage canal. The main drainage drain you will see (GR.880110) has been in use since the marshlands were drained 30 years ago. Look out for water birds and weasels.*

Ride along this bridleway and turn down the second bridleway on the left by the mushroom farm. At the end of this track turn right along another bridleway, and ride up to the bridge (GR.808129) and along Eastoft Moors Drain Road which is a UCR.

Continue along this road until you get to Eastoft. *Here you can enjoy the distant views of Burton on Stather and The Cliff on your right.* **Follow the road through Eastoft to the B1392 and turn left. Continue along this road until you meet the A161 where you turn left. Although this is a main road it is very quiet. Ride along the A161 for about one mile until you come to the double bends. Take the bridleway on your right which is by a big tree (GR.782141).** *At the end of this bridleway you will see more part of the disused railway, including a narrow brick bridge which used to carry trains (GR.775143)!*

20

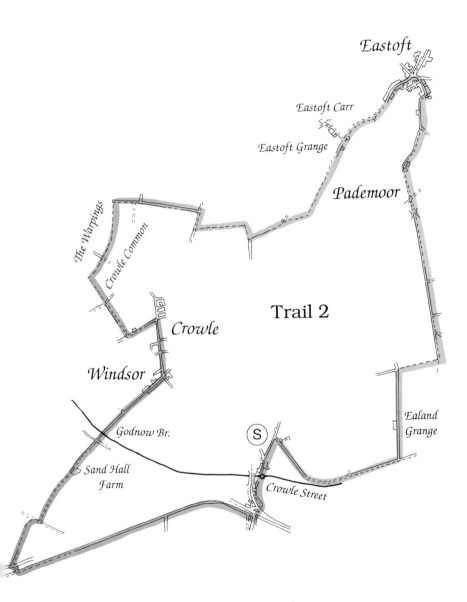

Eastoft

Eastoft Carr

Eastoft Grange

Pademoor

The Warpings

Crowle Common

Trail 2

Crowle

Windsor

Godnow Br.

S

Ealand
Grange

Sand Hall
Farm

Crowle Street

When you reach a road, turn right and follow it to a T-junction where you turn left. Carry on riding along this road until you come to the bridleway which takes you on to Crowle Moors. Take this track and continue riding straight down it ignoring the bridleways you will see on your left. At the end of the sandy track, turn left along the peat track. *On your right is Crowle Peat Works (GR.759145) and the moors which stretch to Thorne Wastes.*

When you come to a T-junction of the UCR, turn left. Ride along this road until you come to a bridleway on your right and turn right on to it. Turn left over the wooden bridge - which is waymarked as a bridleway, and follow the well defined path to Marsh Road. Turn left here. *On your right is the Soldenella Welsh Mountain Pony Stud Farm (GR.768129).* At the end of Marsh Road turn right along Windsor Road.

When you reach the end of Windsor Road, turn right along Godnow Road and follow this to the railway and canal crossing. Cross the canal on the swing bridge (GR.761114) and continue riding straight on along the bridleway.

Keep looking for, and follow, the blue waymarkers - the bridleway turns right at the T-junction of tracks and then left along a headland, with a drainage ditch on your left. Cross the ditch at the little bridge and ride along the next headland keeping the hedge on your right to Smaque Farm (GR.750099). You will now meet the A18.

Cross straight over the A18 with great care - it is very busy but the visibility is good - and continue along the bridleway to meet a road where you turn left. Ride along the road using the good verges to

the left. *Watch out for the water birds along here.*

Just before you reach a main road you will see a stone bridge to your left. Ride across this bridge. *You must now proceed with CAUTION this is a dual carriageway.*

Cross the dual carriageway with great care and ride straight on, past the haulage contractors on your left (GR.782106). It appears that you are heading for a dead-end, however keep riding along the track as there is a tarmac track at the end which takes you on to the top of Crowle flyover. Cross the flyover and at the bottom of the hill, turn right into Ealand.

At the War Memorial, turn left (GR.784112), pass The New Trent Public House and ride back along Wharf Road and so return to your parking place.

HUGGATE

TRAIL 3

A 25 MILE CIRCULAR TRAIL (CLOCKWISE)

Ordnance Survey Map:
Landranger: 106

Parking & Starting Point:
Parking is available by prior arrangement with Mrs Prince at Warren Farm, Warter (GR.840520) - telephone 01759 304091. A small fee will be charged for parking. Please approach the farm via the B1246 **NOT** Millington Village.

Route Description:

Leave the farm and ride along the drive to the road. Turn left and ride 0.75 miles to a T-junction where you turn left (GR.854523). Ride along this road for one mile, passing a farm on the left. When you come to a small cottage on the right, turn left and ride along a well defined bridleway (GR.858537). Ride on until you come to a small wood where you go through the hunting gate to the right and into the old pasture in a valley. The bridleway passes due left alongside the fence at the top of the valley.

Continue to ride following the fence line, all the way to the corner where you turn right and go down the steep hill, still with the fence to your left. Turn left and follow the bridleway signs until you meet the road (GR.848540).

At the road, turn right and ride 0.25 miles going round a bend, pass a 'quarried gap' and turn left (GR.850545) onto a bridleway which takes you into pasture land. Follow this flat-bottomed dry dale to a wooded area. Keeping to the right of the wood, follow the bridleway as the valley narrows and at a division of the track amongst trees, turn right (GR.851565) up the way marked bridleway and ride up hill to meet the road. Ride straight ahead up the lane which is signposted 'Fridaythorpe'.

When you come to the farm buildings, just before the A166, turn right (GR.858577) heading south east, and follow this headland bridleway across one farm drive and on until it meets a second farm drive. This next section is part of the Wolds Way Long Distance Footpath (Permissive riding only through the farm) and passes through Glebe Farm. *Please ride with care and keep off the mown grass.*

Ride through the farm and out down the East Farm drive following the waymarkers. When you meet the lane (GR.881557), turn left and ride 0.75 miles and then take a bridleway which is on the left (GR.885567). Ride to a small gate in the hedge. Go through the gate and ride diagonally right down the hill to the cattle pens and gate. Go through the bridlegate and follow the Wolds

Fridaythorpe

Huggate Wold

North F

Greenwick

Cold Skin

Trail 3

Huggate

Minster Way

Huggate Heads

Cobdale Farm

Cold Wold

Warren
Farm

S

Coldwold Farm

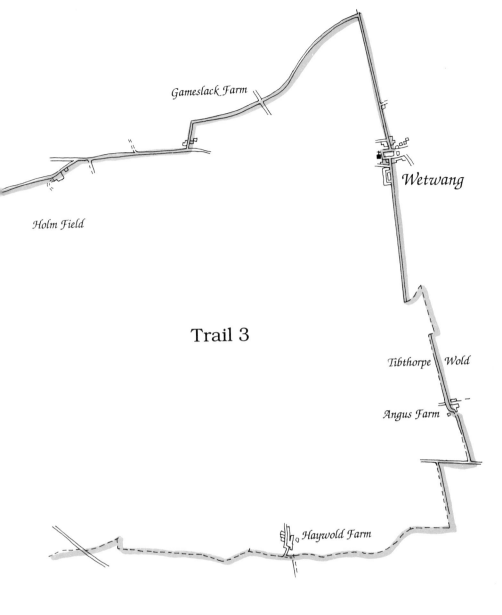

Gameslack Farm

Wetwang

Holm Field

Trail 3

Tibthorpe Wold

Angus Farm

Haywold Farm

Way signs along this wonderful valley. Exit through the five barred gate and then almost immediately turn right (GR.875584) along an old clay road which you should follow for 1.50 miles to meet the A166. Keep right at this road junction.

Exit with care onto the road, visibility is good. Ride for one mile to a roadside farm on the left (GR.909591). Turn left onto the bridleway which takes you through this farm, becoming a wide grass road. Continue on this track for almost two miles, crossing straight over the one road you will encounter.

When you meet the second road, turn right and ride on the road to Wetwang village. When you come to the pub and village pond, turn right and then almost immediately turn left going down the side of the church. Follow the road left and then take the next turn right. Ride on past the houses where the road deteriorates to become a well defined track.

Follow this track for about one mile until it turns left (GR.936573) and then right. *Take care here as there is another bridleway which goes straight on.*

Follow the waymarkers through to Angus Farm, passing a small pond on the way. Ride down the drive from the farm to meet the road (GR.943555). Turn right and ride 0.25 miles to take the bridleway to the left. Ride down a field headland to the trees at the bottom. Turn right (GR.941547) and stay in the bottom going straight ahead and through a gate ignoring the bridleway to the left.

Follow this glorious old grassy route for about seven miles, crossing straight over two tarmac roads. At the third road and cottage, turn left and retrace your steps to your starting point at Warren Farm.

Sheep pasture view from Wold

The Country Code should be observed by every rider, with great care being taken to keep to the line of the Public Rights of Way particularly when crossing farmland.

INSURANCE:

The BHS recommends that before undertaking any of these routes, both horse and rider be adequately insured against **THIRD PARTY PUBLIC LIABILITY.** Membership of the BHS gives automatic Third Party Insurance with an indemnity of up to £2,000,000.

A 13 MILE CIRCULAR TRAIL (ANTI-CLOCKWISE)

Ordnance Survey Map:
Landranger: 106

Parking & Starting Point:
Parking is available by prior arrangement with Mrs Abu Hamdan at High Belthorpe Livery Yard, Bishop Wilton, (GR.781542) telephone: 01759 368238. A small fee will be charged.

Route Description:

From your parking place, ride down the main drive and onto a metalled road heading north east towards Bishop Wilton village. Ride straight ahead through the village to the Fleece Inn. Turn right (GR.797551) and ride along the lane for just over one mile. *This is along the bottom edge of the Wolds where they drop down to the Vale of York.*

Take the first turn left (GR.802536) to Great Givendale, riding up a steep winding hill. At the top of the hill cross directly across the road and ride down an old bridleway skirting the 12th Century St. Ethelburga's Church which is to the right. *After passing the church, to the right you will see lovely wildlife ponds which were originally dug out of the boggy area by the Vikings, to create carp breeding ponds.* **The bridleway is well defined but there is usually stock running on it right through the valley and on up the hill.**

Take care to keep to the track as there are some unpleasant boggy areas on the hill to the left hand side.

Cross the stream by way of the timber bridge (GR.823535). Go through the gate, up the hill and bear slightly left through another gate to follow the track to Little Givendale Farm. Ride down the drive to the beech trees and the road (GR.827525). At the crossroads cross straight over towards Millington Village and on the outskirts of the village of Millington, turn left.

This is a pleasant village with a delightful squat church. If you wish to visit it, turn right, then keep bearing left to return to the crossroads.

Leave the village by following the sign on the left to Millington Pastures. You will first ride along a wide grass verge giving excellent views across the valley, and then along a short narrow bit of lane. On horseback you can cut across the sharp bend in the road. *To your left is Millington Wood and picnic site - a conservation site owned by Humberside County Council, unfortunately horses are not welcome here.*

Ignore the first bridleway to the left and continue on up the road for 0.25 miles. At this point the old

28

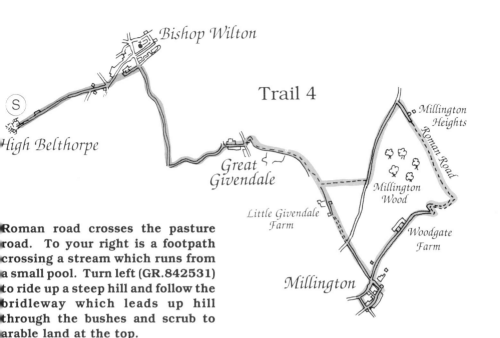

Trail 4

Roman road crosses the pasture road. To your right is a footpath crossing a stream which runs from a small pool. Turn left (GR.842531) to ride up a steep hill and follow the bridleway which leads up hill through the bushes and scrub to arable land at the top.

This is known as 'Thieves Sty' and conjures up visions of all sorts of evil misdeeds. It is also the course of the old Roman road.

Ride straight ahead to the farm and then down the drive to the road, passing the other end of the Millington Wood bridleway to your left.

At the road (GR.834545), turn left and then after 0.75 miles, take the headland bridleway to your right (GR.830533) and follow it to the stone track where you turn right (GR.823533). You will now recognise this area from your outward journey. Retrace your steps back to High Belthorpe enjoying the views going down the hill from Great Givendale.

Wolds Church, Givendale

A 21 MILE CIRCULAR TRAIL (ANTI-CLOCKWISE)

Ordnance Survey Map:
Landranger: 106

Parking & Starting Point:
Parking is available at Warren Farm, Warter, (GR.840520) by prior arrangement with Mrs Prince, telephone 01759 304091. There will be a small charge for parking. Please approach Warren Farm via the B1246 and NOT Millington village. This is also your starting point.

Of Interest:

Warter Village: According to William Thurlows book 'Yorkshire Place Names', this is a compound of the Old English WEARG - a felon and TREOW - a tree, meaning 'The Gallows'. On one side of the green are four lovely thatched cottages, most unusual for this area. This is still an estate village of the Warter estate, formerly owned by Charles Henry Wilson the first Lord Nunburnholme who owned the largest privately owned fleet of Merchant ships in the world and who lived at Warter Priory which was demolished in 1972.

Route Description:

From your parking place, ride back along the farm drive to the lane and turn left. Ride for 0.75 miles to the T-junction and turn left (GR.854524). Ride for one mile passing a farm on the left and then, when you come to a small cottage on the right, turn left along a well defined bridleway (GR.858537). Continue on until you come to a small wood and go through a hunt gate to the right and into old pasture in a valley. The bridleway passes due left along the line of the fence at the top of the valley.

Continue to ride all the way alongside the fence, enjoying the lovely views to the right and straight ahead. When you reach the corner of the fence, turn right and ride down the steep hill, still keeping the fence on your left. Turn left, following the bridleway signs, to the road (GR.848540).

At the road, turn left. Follow the road down the valley to Millington village. *If you look to your left, high on the hill you will see your starting point.*

In Millington village, take the first turn left (GR.831520) and follow the street going past the pub to take the next turn left (GR.830517). The road goes round a right-hand bend, a left-hand bend and then uphill. At the third bend, leave the road and ride straight ahead up the farm drive to Warrendale Farm (GR.831503). *This is a bridleway and also the Wolds Way.* **Go through the farm following the waymarker along the headlands and through gate by a wood, following the track until you come to the B1246.** *To your right you will see the lake and Kilnwic*

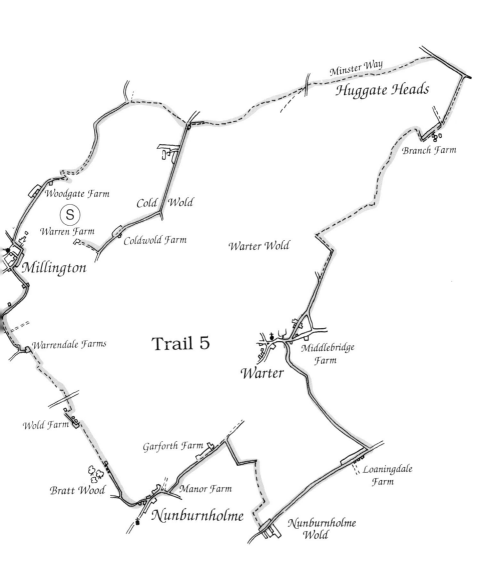

Minster Way

Huggate Heads

Branch Farm

Woodgate Farm

Cold Wold

(S)

Warren Farm

Coldwold Farm

Warter Wold

Millington

Warter

Middlebridge Farm

Trail 5

Warrendale Farms

Wold Farm

Garforth Farm

Loaningdale Farm

Bratt Wood

Manor Farm

Nunburnholme

Nunburnholme Wold

Percy Hall which is a Buddhist retreat.

When you come to the B1246, go through the gate and straight across the road. *Take care here, visibility up the hill is restricted and the traffic can be fast.* **Follow the bridleway as it turns up through Wold Farm- you may encounter pigs along the driveway!**

As you leave the farm, you can enjoy the spectacular views to the right across the Vale of York. The three power stations are Drax, Eggborough and Ferrybridge and on a clear day it is possible to see the outline of the Pennines and York Minster.

Continue to ride on over the hill going through pasture land and down through Bratt Wood to the road (GR.846482). Turn left along the road and ride through Nunburnholme village, following the road to the right, over a small bridge and stream. After crossing the bridge over the stream, take the first left turn (GR.853483), signposted Warter. Follow this road for just under one mile and take the bridleway to the right which is a chalk track running uphill (GR.863489). Ride along this track and into the woods going up the cart track which is just inside the eastern side of the woods. This is well defined and waymarked all the way to the road at Nunburnholme Wold Farm (GR.867477).

Turn left along the road. *Note the wonderful scenery of Londesborough Estates to your right.* **Take the next road turning left, signposted Warter (GR.884487). When you come to the village, cross the B1246 with care and turn right past the pond and then immediately turn left (GR.873504) up the road leading out of the village.**

Ride along this road for 0.75 miles to a clearly marked bridleway on the right which goes along a green lane. It does an odd zig-zag almost back to the road, but you keep to the right. Skirt around the woods and then turn right and go through a hunt gate and into old pasture, known as Lavenderdale. *No, there is not any lavender and the landscape is green!!*

Ride straight on down the hill going diagonally left up the other side, along under the hedgeside and then through another gate to follow the waymarkers to Blanch Farm (GR.897534).

The track comes out past a Dutch barn with the farm cottage in front of you. The bridleway is the farm drive to your left and you follow this to the road (GR.901542). Turn left here and after 0.25 miles, take the well defined bridleway to the left (GR.897545). *This is part of the Minster Way Walk.* **Continue on and cross straight over one road.** *Note the head of the beautiful 'Golden Valley' to the left just after the crossing Unfortunately this is not a right of way* **When you come to the second road (GR.858537), turn left and retrace your steps to your parking place.**

Wolds Church

A 14 MILE CIRCULAR TRAIL (CLOCKWISE)

Ordnance Survey Maps:
Landranger: 101 & 106

Parking & Starting Point:
Parking is available for two large horseboxes at the Tatton Sykes Monument (GR.958618). This is also your starting point.

NB: Please do not block this green lane as farm vehicles have access.

Route Description:

From your parking place proceed in a north-easterly direction and cross the tarmac road. Follow the chalk road by the side of the cottage for 1.50 miles, until you come to another road (GR.975628). Turn left and after a short distance take the waymarked bridleway on the right (GR.973634) which goes through a gate and into a field. Follow the waymarking along this valley bottom for about 2 miles, as it curves right to the deserted church at the site of old Cottam village. *Ignore all bridleway markers to the left off this route.* **Leave the bridleway just past the church, by going through the gate on to the lane.**

Immediately cross the lane and skirt right, round the edge of a planting of trees. At the first drive, turn left and ride for 40 yards along the drive and then go right following th waymarking onto the old runway Continue to ride straight ahead to bridleway interchange. Turn righ then left, following the waymarker and across a field into an old 'hedge green road which takes you downhi to Cottam Warren Farm. *This is reclaimed bridleway and is n shown on the current Ordnanc Survey Map.* Ride straight ahead o the tarmac lane.

Another lane will join from the righ You take the first right turn up th drive of Elmswell Wold Far (GR.000610). Ride past the farm t the wide green lane where you tur left (GR.993608) and ride thi glorious grass road to the main A16 (GR.991588). Cross this road wit care and continue to ride straigh ahead. After 0.75 miles, take a obvious turning onto a track on th right (GR.989577). *This is part grass, partly stone and a bit tarmac.* Follow in a straight lin westward for a little over 2 mile Ahead of you and to the right, yo will see some large, low, turke rearing houses. Just before the the track narrows through bushe and you will find a waymarked ga in the hedge to your righ (GR.950580) which will lead yo back to the A166.

Cross the A166, diagonally righ through the iron gate and ride th headland and track towards Garto Field Farm, crossing a chalk roa

on the way. Just before Garton
Fields Farm, the bridleway leads
you left through a gate and up the
east side of a belt of trees
(GR.953607). Follow this bridleway
past the trees, uphill to the grass
drove road. Turn right and so ride
back to the Tatton Sykes Monument
and your starting point.

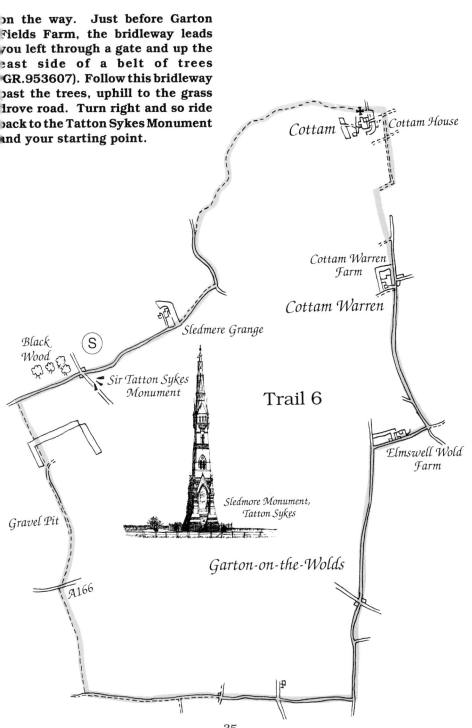

Cottam

Cottam House

*Cottam Warren
Farm*

Cottam Warren

Sledmere Grange

*Black
Wood*

(S)

*Sir Tatton Sykes
Monument*

Trail 6

*Elmswell Wold
Farm*

*Sledmore Monument,
Tatton Sykes*

Gravel Pit

A166

Garton-on-the-Wolds

SALTMARSHE

TRAIL
7

**A 15 MILE CIRCULAR TRAIL
(ANTI-CLOCKWISE)**

Ordnance Survey Map:
Landranger: 106

Parking & Starting Point:
Parking is available near Waterside
House (GR.811236). There is room on
the verges to park one or two boxes,
but **DO NOT** park at the farm itself.

Of Interest:
*This is a circular route in North
Humberside, south east of the market
town of Howden. It is a flat easy ride
encompassing quiet lanes and
bridleways with views of the River
Ouse.*

Route Description:

**From your parking point, ride north
up the lane you have just come down
to park your transport. At the road
junction (GR.809249), turn left and
ride along the lane through the scenic
village of Laxton.** *Laxton takes its
name from the Norse word 'Lax' meaning
salmon which swam in the nearby river.*

**Cross over the railway line by way of
the manned level crossing
(GR.786258) and one mile after the
crossing, the road turns left 90
degrees, here you must turn right
down the waymarked grass bridleway
(GR.777263).**

**Follow this green lane for just over
two miles to come to the tarmac**

road in the village of Balkholme
**Ride through Balkholme until you
come to a T-junction (GR.783282)
Turn left and follow the lane to the
village of Kilpin. Ignore the road
turning to your right and continue
on until the road takes a sharp left
turn, where you must turn right
onto the bridleway which will take
you across the south side of the old
farm buildings (GR.772266).**

**You are now travelling roughly in a
westerly direction along a field
headland.** *Directly in front of you you
can see the timber works at Kilpin Pike
When you reach the timber works and
the road, the River Ouse is immediately
front of you over the flood dyke.*

**At the road, turn left (GR.761266
and ride along with the river on you
right for approximately 1.50 miles
You will now see a railway
embankment in front of you. DO
NOT ride under at this point, instead
turn left and ride along the tarmac
lane and under another railway arch
(GR.772248) which is 0.75 mile
further along the tarmac road.** *You
will notice the conservation pond t
your left.* **Continue to ride on into
Saltmarshe Park.**

Ride through the park. *The Ha
clearly visible on your right.* **Stil
keeping to the road, ride directly
through the village of Saltmarshe
keeping the river to your right. Th
road ahead becomes a track and the
a bridleway (GR.795241).**

36

You will now be travelling in an easterly direction and will come to a very large field drain (GR.798242). Turn left here and then almost immediately turn right over a grass topped brick bridge. Ride straight ahead through the bridgegate which leads you into pasture land. *Please be sure and close the gate after you.*

Continue to ride directly ahead (*not towards the farm on your right*) and you will see a bridlegate in the corner of the field. This leads you onto the road (GR.799241).

Cross the road diagonally to the right and ride to the end of the barn. Go through another bridlegate and into more pasture. Ride diagonally across the field and out through the gate - *closing it behind you.* Ride straight ahead and follow the clearly defined track back to Waterside House and your starting point.

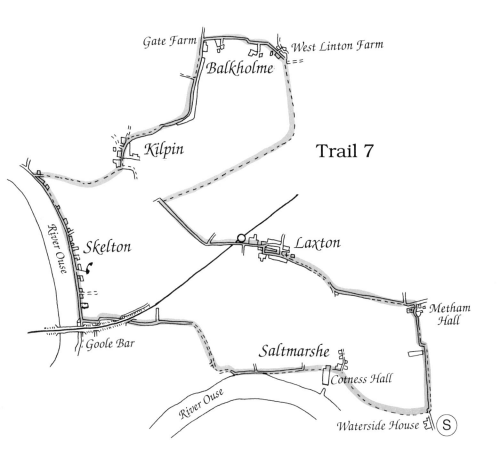

WOLD NEWTON- SOUTH HUMBERSIDE

TRAIL 8

HUMBERSIDE
A 15 MILE CIRCULAR TRAIL
(CLOCKWISE)

Ordnance Survey Map:
Landranger: 113

Parking & Starting Point:
Parking is available on the grass verge
0.50 miles north of Cold Harbour Farm,
Swinhope Brats (GR.231953).

Of Interest:
*This is a circular route in South
Humberside, crossing and re-crossing
the Lincolnshire County border, west of
the A18 close to the charming village of
Wold Newton. It is an undulating and
scenic ride of quiet lanes and well
marked bridleways over chalk wold
land.*

Route Description:

From your parking place ride in a
northerly direction taking the first
road on the left to come to a T-
junction (GR.226964) where you
turn left. Follow this road and take
the second turning on the right
(GR.218960) and continue along this
road until it turns 90 degrees to the
left (GR.210960).   Turn right
following the waymarkers past the
agricultural works and follow the
tracks into the woods.

Take the lesser track going to the
left in the middle of the woods when
the track divides and then where it
breaks out, turn right. Straight ahead
across the fields you can clearly see

the chalk road which you must ride
to meet.

On meeting the chalk road, follow it
northwards to come out near
Thorganby village.   Turn right
(GR.206977) and ride for 150 yards.
You will now see a lane on the left
which you must turn along
(GR.207977). This lane is quiet and
has wide, flat verges which you follow
to woodland. Still on the same road
ride down the hill and when you see
the waymarked bridleway and gate
to the right (GR.201998) turn and go
through the gate.

Follow the bridleway straight ahead
to come to a stream.   Cross the
stream going over the bridge and
keep riding straight ahead through
the grasses to exit from the bridleway
via a bridlegate which is clearly
marked to the left at the end of a
stand of larch trees.

From this gate, follow the track to
the next gate along a well defined
headland track with a hedge on your
left. After passing through this gate
turn immediately right along the
waymarked track and follow it to
meet the road where you exit through
the large farm gates. Turn left along
the road (GR.215003) and then
almost immediately turn right going
round the cattle grid and follow a
pretty road through West Ravendale
to East Ravendale.

Ride directly across the road

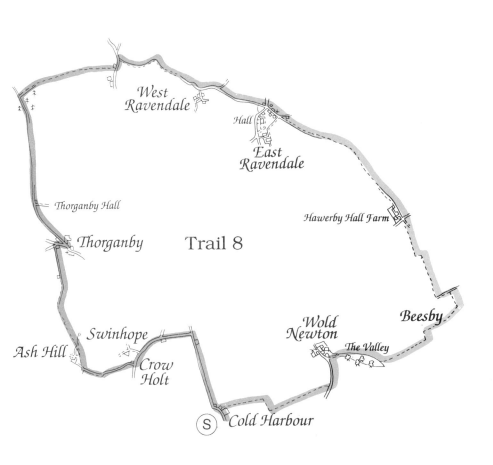

West
Ravendale

Hall

East
Ravendale

Thorganby Hall

Hawerby Hall Farm

Thorganby

Trail 8

Beesby

Wold
Newton

The Valley

Swinhope

Ash Hill

Crow
Holt

(S) Cold Harbour

Wolds view

39

(GR.237997) and ride straight ahead passing a small wood on the right. At the fence and T-junction turn right and follow the track to the end of the wood on your left. Follow the waymarkers left and you will soon bear left up a grassy headland with the hedge to your right. Follow the hedge to a wide gap and track on the right and turn along this track following the waymarkers.

Ride straight ahead passing Hawerby Hall Farm to the lane. Cross straight across following a well worn track. You will have the hedge on your right and you follow the track to a small gate in the hedge. Go through the gate, turn left and skirt the gardens to the lane. Turn left along the lane and ride for 150 yards and turn right following the waymarks. With the hedge on your right ride straight ahead, until you leave the end of the hedge and ride 250 yards straight ahead on a grassy bank. At the farm track turn left and take the next bridleway right which leads to the woods above Beesby hamlet (GR.266968).

With the woods in front of you, turn right and follow a well defined grass track which skirts the woods and bears left to go through a gate at the end. Having gone through the gate, bear right and follow the next section which is well waymarked, but has quite a few gates. *Take care - there are a number of rabbit holes but they are large and clearly visible.*

Follow this track and the waymarkers to the next section of woodland known as 'The Valley'. Following the waymarkers, turn into the woodland and follow the track through the woods down to meet a road. Exit

round the gates and you are now south of the village of Wold Newton. Turn left (GR.246961) and ride along the road, turning right onto the waymarked bridleway which is a grassy track (GR.247956).

Continue to follow the waymarkers in a westerly direction back to the road at Cold Harbour and turn right up the road to return to your transport.

Flamborough Head

HORNSEA

A 13 MILE CIRCULAR TRAIL (ANTI-CLOCKWISE)

Ordnance Survey Map:
Landranger: 107

Parking & Starting Point:
Parking on this route is limited and it is suggested that you use the wide grass verge on the Goxhill Road which is due east of Sigglesthorne village (GR.167455). Alternative parking is available, by prior arrangement only, slightly further north at Bewholme. Please telephone 01964 533739 - a small fee will be charged for parking.

Of Interest:
This is a circular route in North Humberside. It is close to the seaside resort of Hornsea. The route is bridleways, quiet lanes and the Hornsea Rail trail - a Humberside County Council recreational green corridor. The going is mostly flat with scenic views on the northern side to Hornsea Mere.

Route Description:

From your parking place ride south along the lane until it takes a sharp left turn 90 degrees. Your ride continues straight ahead down a well defined farm track which is waymarked as a bridleway.

On meeting the next tarmac road, turn left (GR.162440) and almost immediately turn right. Still on tarmac, look for a bridleway marker on the left (GR.154435) which takes

you on a well used route to the estate village of Rise. As you approach the village, turn left down the waymarked clay lane which leads onto a long headland bridleway which meets a bridleway junction. At this junction, turn right and after 1.50 miles of bridleway riding, you will meet a road. Turn left and ride along the grass verge to the old Hull to Hornsea railway line which is now a recreational trail.

Turn left (GR.173409) onto the trail and follow it in a north easterly direction for almost five miles crossing three tarmac roads. *Note after the first road, the route leaves the track bed and uses the right hand embankment for a short stretch of the way.*

When the road starts to enter a steep cutting, (GR.195455) exit to the left up the embankment to the top of the cutting and follow a narrow track along the top to the road at the bridge (GR.198459). *The bridleway markers themselves are incongruous and would take you up a flight of steps instead!*

On the road, with the railway and bridge to your right, turn left (GR.198459) and ride along the verge to the first lane on the left (GR.197462).

Ride along this lane and you will see a waymark in the trees which gives you a clear route to follow in an ar

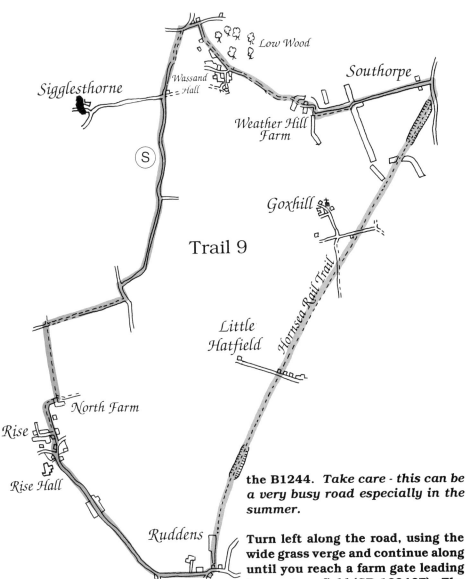

Trail 9

round the south and west side of **Hornsea Mere.** *There are several gates in this section, but it is exceptionally pretty with the views of the Mere through the trees.*

You will now come out on the drive of Wassand Hall which is also a bridleway and this will lead you onto

the B1244. *Take care - this can be a very busy road especially in the summer.*

Turn left along the road, using the wide grass verge and continue along until you reach a farm gate leading into a grass field (GR.169467). The route across the field is a clear chalk track. Ride along it and out of the next farm gate at the bottom of the wood. *There are usually cattle in this field.* **The track may not be marked as a bridleway as it is in fact an Unclassified County Road. Once you have passed through this bottom gate, return via the green lane to the road and so back to the start.**

43

A 15 MILE CIRCULAR TRAIL (CLOCKWISE)

Ordnance Survey Map:
Landranger: 101

Parking & Starting Point:
Ample good parking is available by prior arrangement with Mr & Mrs Keyes at Eastgate Cottage, Woldgate, Kilham (GR.074645) telephone: 01262 420358. A small fee will be charged.

Of Interest:
This is a scenic ride along the edge of the Wolds with stunning views across the Plain of Holderness and far away to sea.

Route Description:

From your parking place turn left. Ride gradually uphill on the good verges along the old Roman road. Continue for about 2.50 miles going past the road turn to Rudston which is on the left. Stay straight ahead where it is signposted Bridlington. *Pause and enjoy the splendid views to your right of the Plain of Holderness and in the distance, the North Sea.* **You will see ahead a radio mast. Approximately 250 yards before the mast, look for and take, the wide bridleway on the left (GR.107660). Follow this bridleway for 0.75 miles and bear left with it into Rudston village.**

At the village road, turn right and almost immediately go right (GR.095673) **again along Eastgate. Follow this road bearing left into Church Lane and to the church.**

Rudston is Neolithic in origin and believed to be the oldest inhabited village in England. The church has 12th century chancel and Norman tower. Winifred Holtby, the authoress of 'South Riding' is buried in the churchyard, where you will also find the famous Monolith or Rood-stone from which the village takes its name. It stands at the meeting place of four Neolithic ditches coming from the four main compass points. Standing 2 feet 4 inches high, the nearest similar type of stone is ten miles away at Cayton on the coast.

Facing the church, from Church Lane, turn right and ride on to the B1253 (GR.098678). Turn right passing the War Memorial on the left. Ride along the B1253 which is not usually busy. Go past the first bridleway, which is chalk road, and 0.50 miles further on, almost opposite a campsite, turn left (GR.106677), heading north, onto a bridleway which you should follow for one mile. The bridleway ends at a tarmac farm drive where you turn right (GR.107693) and ride along the drive, following the trail all the way to High Caythorpe Farm. Ride straight through the farm. Ignore any other waymarkers to the left and right.

After the farm, the lane becomes

clearly defined track which goes to, and alongside, the north side of a small wood and on to meet a metalled road.

At the road, turn right (GR.131705) heading south, and ride on into Boynton village. *The verge is very good until just before the village where the road narrows.* Ride straight across the B1253 (GR.136682) and continue for about 300 yards. Look for, and take, the waymarked bridleway on the right (GR.136680). This leads uphill past the farm to the road. *At the time of writing, this bridleway is the subject of a current diversion order and so it may appear different to the Ordnance Survey Map.*

At the road, cross onto the bridleway which lies amongst the trees. This track becomes a stony surface going through a long tunnel of trees. When the track meets the road (GR.138660), turn left and almost immediately, turn right onto a clay track. Follow this track passing the concrete poles on your right. Further on, the main track becomes tarmac and bears right up to Woldgate, the old Roman Road (GR.121664).

Turn left onto the road and follow it all the way back to Kilham and your starting point.

BURTON PIDSEA

TRAIL 11

A 12 or 15 MILE CIRCULAR TRAIL (CLOCKWISE)

Ordnance Survey Map:
Landranger: 107

Parking & Starting Point:
Parking is available in the Village Hall Car Park at Burton Pidsea (GR.250310), which is a scenic village lying to the east of Kingston upon Hull.

Route Description:

From your parking place, ride west along the back lane of Burton Pidsea, turning right (GR.244311) into Jubilee Lane. Continue on until you come to a T-junction (GR.244314) and turn left to ride along the main road for a short distance, going over a bridge and taking the turn to the right (GR.243315) which is signposted to Danthorpe. *The verge here is well used and the lane is quiet.*

At the White Cottages (GR.240325) turn left and follow the clearly defined bridleway that takes you down a short green lane, past farm buildings, through two bridlegates and over a stream to come to St Lawrence Church at Elstronwick. Continue to ride straight ahead past the Crown & Anchor Public House. Having passed the Crown & Anchor, take the second turning on the right (GR.225321) which will take you towards the old windmill.

Just past the windmill on the left look for and follow the signposted

bridleway which will take you across a grass field, usually containing stock, through two gates and then onto a waymarked headland which will take you to meet a road (GR.212322). Turn right at the road.

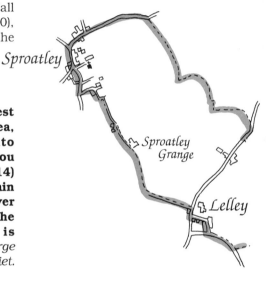

Sproatley

Sproatley Grange

Lelley

You will see from your map that there are two ways to go through the village of Lelley, but you turn right (GR.209324) on the outskirts. This misses out most of the traffic and will bring you out on the north side of The Stag Inn. Here you turn right onto the Humbleton road and ride for just a few yards past the cottages on the left and then turn immediately left (GR.208328) along the side of the last cottage to ride along the waymarked bridleway. Follow this track which will take you straight through Sproatley Grange to the village of Sproatley.

The traffic in Sproatley is not usually large or fast. **When you come to the junction of the B1240 and B1238, turn right (GR.192344) towards Aldbrough and follow the road for about 0.75 miles going out of the village and turn right onto the well defined byway (GR.202350).** *There are several sharp turns but the way is apparent.*

Follow this byway until it meets the road where you turn right (GR.215336) and then almost immediately, go left and ride back along the road to Elstronwick Mill. From the Mill you retrace your steps back to Burton Pidsea Village Hall

Car Park. *This is the finish of the 12 mile trail, if you wish to do the 15 mile ride then continue as follows:*

Pass the Car Park and your starting point and turn right (GR.250310). Ride past the 'No Through Road' signs and you will see a clearly defined clay road known locally as Mucky Lane. This is marked as a bridleway on your right (GR.253309). Turn along here and follow the track for about a mile when you will find it suddenly bends to the left and then divides. Take the left turn and follow the well defined track to Elm Tree Farm (GR.261296) which stands on the edge of the low lying Carrs.

Ride past the front of the farm and on along the lane to return to the village and your parking place.

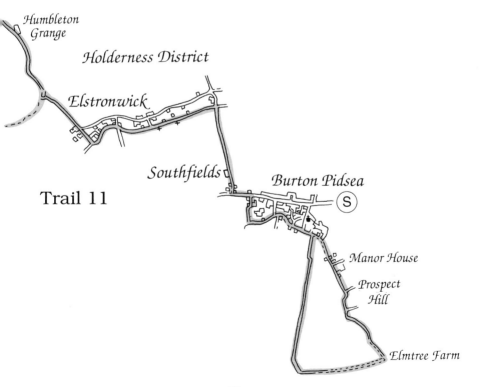

Trail 11

A 20 MILE CIRCULAR TRAIL (ANTI-CLOCKWISE)

Ordnance Survey Map:
Landranger: 112

Parking & Starting Point:
Parking is available in lay-bys on the A161, north of Eastoft. There is room in either for about four cars with trailers. (GR.806206 or GR.809204).

Route Description:

From your parking place, head south-east along a good grass verge on the left hand side of the A161 towards Eastoft. The road is not busy. At the sharp bend, take the waymarked bridleway on the left. Follow the main track past the farm buildings and continue straight on where another bridleway joins from the left (GR.819208).

After 0.50 miles you will come to a T-junction of bridleways (GR.824200). Turn right and follow the blue waymarkers. When you meet the road (A161), turn left. Using the good grass verges, stay on the road for about one mile until you come to the bridleway at Boltgate Farm (GR.810177). The bridleway follows the headland keeping the hedge on the right until it reaches a cart track. Continue along this track to Luddington where you turn left at the road (GR.827164) onto the B1392.

At the right-angle bend on the B1392, head east staying on the road until you come to the river bank at Mere Dyke Cottage (GR.850167). *Here you will have some splendid views of Luddington's spired church which is on your left.* At Mere Dyke Cottage turn left, and follow the road to Garthorpe, again using the good wide grass verges on the right. *To your left you will see Waterton Hall (GR.853179), which is the sole survivor of the medieval settlement of Waterton. At the sharp left-hand bend in the road, look at the old slipway track. This used to lead to Garthorpe Ferry which crossed the River Trent to Burton Stather.*

When you come to the cross roads in Garthorpe, turn left (GR.848192). Go past the church on your right and continue through the village. When the road bends sharply to the left, you must continue to ride straight on along the minor road to Fockerby. At the end of this road turn right and then left on to the Unclassified County Road (GR.844191).

Follow this well defined road, taking the main left turn under the pylon lines, to Willowbank Bridge which crosses the Adlingfleet Drain (GR.832196). Cross the bridge on to the bridleway and ride to the end of the lane. Continue riding along the headland and follow the bridleway into Adlingfleet.

48

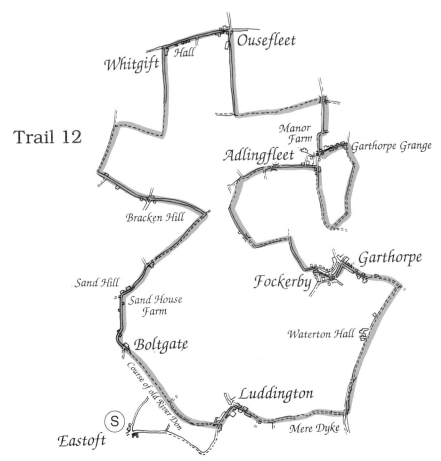

Trail 12

Whitgift
Hall
Ousefleet
Manor
Farm
Adlingfleet
Garthorpe Grange
Bracken Hill
Sand Hill
Sand House
Farm
Boltgate
Garthorpe
Fockerby
Waterton Hall
Course of old River Don
Luddington
S
Eastoft
Mere Dyke

Ride past the Post Office to a T-junction (GR.844208) where you turn right. Continue along this road for about 0.50 miles and take the bridleway on your left (GR.848198). Follow this well defined path to Garthorpe Grange (GR.849212).

When you meet the road, turn left and ride into Adlingfleet again, this time to the T-junction opposite the splendid towered church. Turn right out of the village and along the road. As soon as you have crossed the bridge, turn left on to the bridleway (GR.845220). Follow the bridleway, going under the pylon lines and turn right along the surfaced Unclassified County Road to Ousefleet.

In Ousefleet, turn left along the road (GR.829232). *Notice the heavy Dutch influence in the style of the buildings.* Continue to ride along the road, past the Post Office on the left, the church on the right and Whitgift Hall (GR.816228). Just after the Hall, turn left along the bridleway. Ride past all the buildings and over the fields. On reaching the road, turn left and ride for about 200 yards to meet the A161. Turn left here (GR.804206) and ride back to the lay-by and your transport.

BRANTINGHAM

A 19 MILE CIRCULAR TRAIL (CLOCKWISE)

Ordnance Survey Maps:
Landranger: 106

Parking & Starting Point:
Parking is available on the wide grass verges just over the A63 bridge to the south-west of Brantingham village. (GR.937291). This is also the start of your ride.

NB: It is possible to shorten this ride to 12 miles and details are given in the text.

Route Details:

From your parking place, ride along the road to the Village War Memorial, then turn left (GR.940293) past the side of the Triton Inn and take the unmarked road turning right (GR.938295). Ride on past the pond and the Hall, bearing left towards the church. From the church stay on the road known as Brantingham Dale Road and ride on to meet a T-junction (GR.958319). *A superb fitness test is to trot from the church all the way up the dale road to the T-junction at the top by Keepers Cottage!* At the T-junction, turn right and continue to a crossroads. *This is a busy road so take CARE. It is best to ride along the verge against the traffic as it is wider and well used by horses.*

At the crossroads turn right (GR.963318) and ride along the good grass verge, again against the traffic and near the hedge. Continue on past Field House Farm and at the bottom turn left (GR.963304) along the track marked Wolds Way. *Please give way to walkers!*

After 0.50 miles*, take the bridleway on the left (GR.972305) up a well marked track, past the farm and cottages to come to a road (GR.976315). With CARE, turn left and almost immediately turn right onto a bridleway. Follow this bridleway to the pylons and bear right to the old railway line. Here turn right (GR.996326) along another well worn bridleway to the top of the golf course. Turn right and follow the track round the golf course to the road. At the road (GR.998310) turn right and ride along to a bend to go through the fence on the left and left again on to the bridleway, riding up the steep hill to the woods at the top.** *This area is known as Wauldby Green and before it was ploughed and fenced in the winter it was a favourite place to toboggan. Opposite you will see Raywell House, which until recently was a Sanatorium.*

Ride on with the woods on the right and at the end, turn left onto a bridleway (GR.985302). Ride to the farm cottage then down the drive to the tarmac road (GR.990293). Turn right and ride for approximately 100 yards and turn right (GR.988291) again along a track

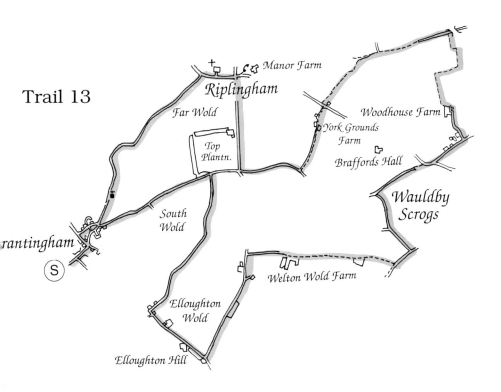

Trail 13

Manor Farm
Riplingham
Far Wold
Woodhouse Farm
York Grounds Farm
Top Plantn.
Braffords Hall
Wauldby Scrogs
South Wold
rantingham
(S)
Welton Wold Farm
Elloughton Wold
Elloughton Hill

which may be muddy. **Follow this bridleway going through the bushes to the top of the hill, and enjoy the wonderful views. Continue riding straight on to meet a road (GR.964292).**

At the road turn left. *You are requested to ride slowly for the next 300 yards until you have passed the riding centre.* **Continue on down the hill to a road junction (GR.058277). Turn right and ride along the wide grass verge for just over a mile going over Welton High Hill and take the next road on the right (GR.950284) up Elloughton Dale. Ignore the bridleway which lies straight ahead and ride on the road up Elloughton Dale and into the open at the top. When the road bears sharp right, take the grass track going left (GR.959304) which**

is marked Wolds Way. **This good green lane suddenly becomes tarmac and goes down a very steep hill known as Spout Hill.**

Enjoy the view as you ride down the hill and back to the village. In the village ride straight ahead keeping the village pump and then the pond, on your right and so back to your starting point.

Alternative:
*If you wish to take the shorter 12 mile ride when you reach * (GR.972305) instead of turning left, continue to ride straight along the bottom of the valley all the way through to the road. Do not go on to the road, but turn right up the hill to come to the woods at the top where your ride continues from ** in the route description.*

51

KIPLINGCOATES

AN 11 MILE CIRCULAR TRAIL (CLOCKWISE)

Ordnance Survey Maps:
Landranger: 106

Parking & Starting Point:
Parking is available on the wide grass verges just east of Goodmanham village (GR.893434). Your ride is described from here.

Of Interest:
Much of the route of this ride is on wide, flat, grass verges. This ride incorporates part of the route of the Kiplingcoates Derby racecourse which is held on the third Thursday in March and is the oldest flat race in the country. Much of the race's length is on the wide grass verges found in abundance in this area.

Route Description:

From your parking place ride into the village and turn right (GR.890432) going past the church and follow the Wolds Way signs. Follow this headland bridleway to come to the A163 (GR.878440) Towthorpe Corner Picnic Site. *Visibility is good and the traffic is slowing down for the roundabout..* From the picnic area, turn left and ride to the roundabout on the wide grass verges beside this 'A' road. Go right (the last exit), TAKING GREAT CARE on this major road and ride towards Londesborough village. As you approach the village you ride around the outskirts of the delightful park to the right.

This village has a wonderful history, being in the ownership of the Burlington family and Devonshire family. In 1848 it was bought by George Hudson the 'Railway King'. The Hall was long since demolished, but the village proper is little changed except for the careful conversion of existing buildings.

At the T-junction turn right (GR.865454) and then take the second turning left (GR.866455) which has good verges and superb views across the Vale of York. Follow this lane for about one mile, heading north, to a crossroads where you turn right (GR.863472) along the road which takes you over Nunburnholme Wold. Ride for about two miles on this quiet road. *Take time to admire the scenery which includes the Londesborough Estate in the valley to the right.*

Look for, and ride past, Loaningdale Farm and take the road on the right (GR.888489) heading south. Follow the road down a dip and up to the woods at the top. *Here you will notice a white post in a gateway to your left this is the finishing post of the Kiplingcoates race.* Keep riding straight ahead to meet the A163 (GR.897475) which you cross with care to continue on down the clay track of the racecourse. This becomes a chalk road which you continue along to the top of the Enthorpe House drive. Here you turn right (GR.918457) and ride along the wide grass verge all the way back to Goodmanham village and you parking place.

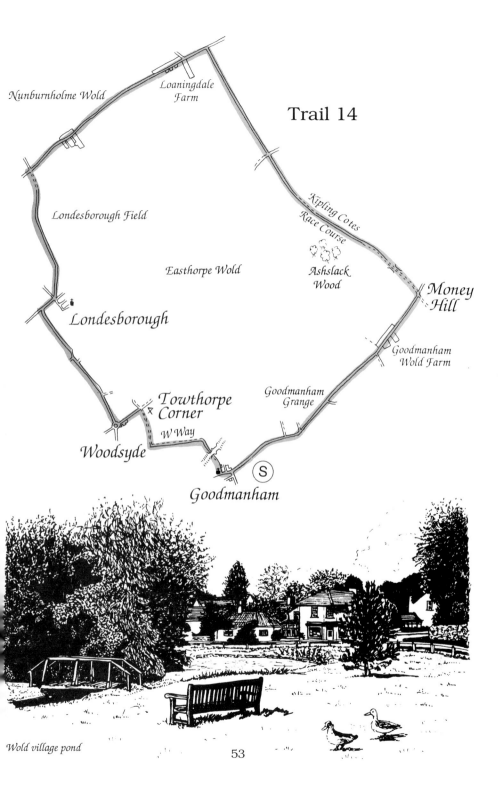

Trail 14

Nunburnholme Wold

Loaningdale
Farm

Londesborough Field

Kipling Cotes
Race Course

Easthorpe Wold

Ashslack
Wood

Money
Hill

Londesborough

Goodmanham
Wold Farm

Goodmanham
Grange

Towthorpe
Corner

W Way

Woodsyde

Ⓢ

Goodmanham

Wold village pond

53

A 11 MILE CIRCULAR TRAIL (ANTI-CLOCKWISE)

Ordnance Survey Map:
Landranger: 106

Parking & Starting Point:
Parking is available at the Northern Shire Horse Centre, Flower Hill Farm at Newbald (GR.935384) by prior arrangement with Angela Cammidge. Telephone: (01430) 827480). This is also the starting point for your ride.

Of Interest:
Newbald is an interesting little settlement. Roman remains have been found nearby but the place was first mentioned in the 10th Century when the Saxon King Edgar granted land rights. The Danes then occupied the area and Ulphus, son-in-law of the famous King Canute dedicated the lands to God and they passed into the ownership of the Church. Newbald boasts a fine Norman church built of local stone.

The Bishop in the village name of Bishop Burton, comes from the Archbishops of York who had a palace within the parish and in 1296 Archbishop Romanus died there. Burton is found in many place names in the area and means 'fortified place'.

Route Description:

From Flower Hill Farm drive, turn left and ride down the roadside verge towards the village of Newbald and turn left at the road junction (GR.922373). Follow this lane passing the back of Flower Hill Farm and ride for about 5 miles, where possible using the good rideable verges. Take the first left turning (GR.987382) towards Bishop Burton, heading north.

At the outskirts of the village look for and turn along, a bridleway and metalled road to the left (GR.987397).

It is worth noticing the village which is home to the Agricultural College, has a delightful assortment of white cottages and a large village pond teeming with ducks. The strangely named pub is named after a St Leger winner 'Altisidora' and is visible across the main road, but it is inadvisable to try and get to it with horses due to the thundering traffic on the A1079.

Follow the well defined bridleway as it leaves the village and gently climbs Bishop Burton Wold to Newbald Lodge Farm. Cross the road (GR.942397) and take the bridleway to the rear of the farm which follows headlands for about one mile. When you come to the next road (GR.938401), turn immediately left down another bridleway, which is known as Heselskewgare and is part of the Wolds Way. At the next road (GR.929381) turn left and ride along the wide verges back to your parking place at the Northern Shire Horse Centre at Flower Hill Farm.

54

Trail 15

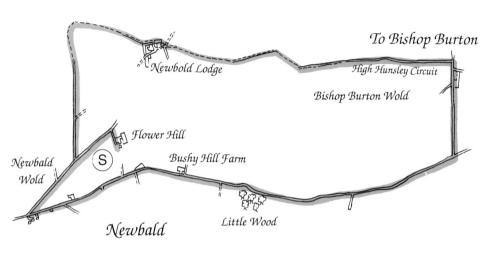

To Bishop Burton

Newbold Lodge

High Hunsley Circuit

Bishop Burton Wold

Flower Hill

Newbald Wold

S

Bushy Hill Farm

Newbald

Little Wood

Wolds landscape

Disclaimer

Whilst all due care was taken in the preparation of these maps neither the British Horse Society nor their agents or servants accept any responsibility for any inaccuracies which may occur. It should be borne in mind that landmarks and conditions change and it is assumed that the user has a Pathfinder or Landranger Ordnance Survey map and a compass.

The Country Code should be observed by every rider, with great care being taken to keep to the line of the Public Rights of Way particularly when crossing farmland.

56

(20 OR 25 MILE CIRCULAR TRAIL ANTI-CLOCKWISE)

Ordnance Survey Maps:
Landranger: 106

Parking & Starting Point:
Parking is available at the Northern Shire Horse Centre at Newbald (GR.935384). Although there is ample parking, please telephone Angela Cammidge (01430) 827480 to confirm he has space.

Route Details:

From your parking place, ride up the drive to meet a road at the end. Turn left and ride downhill along the verge until you come to a green lane on the right (GR.929381), which is a bridleway. Turn right here, heading north, and ride uphill along this green lane enjoying the lovely views of true chalk wold landscapes. At the top of this lane you will meet a road where you will see a bridleway immediately to the right (GR.928401). Take this bridleway and follow around the headlands on the north side of the farm to meet the road at Newbald Lodge. Turn left (GR.943397) along this unfenced lane to meet the A1079 (GR.949412). *Cross this road with care. Visibility is good and there is plenty of room for horses on the verge, but the traffic is fast.*

Ride on along the unfenced lane down to Gardham and after passing the farm on the left, take the well used bridleway (GR.955424) which goes under the railway line and up past Etton West Wood to meet a road (GR.952437). Turn left here along the wide grass verge.

NB: *From here the map shows road work, but in reality the route takes you along very wide, flat grass verges which are well ridden and used to train the local point-to-point horses!!*

Cross straight over the first cross roads (GR.941440). *Just past the planting on the right you will notice a stone set upright in the verge. This is the starting point of the Kiplingcoates Derby, which is held on the third Thursday in March and is the oldest flat race in the country and the verge you are riding on **IS** the race track.*

Continue riding straight on crossing the second crossroads (GR.932445). *On race day the police stop the traffic here.* **At the top of the hill, the verge virtually disappears and the 'official' racetrack continues ahead down the drive of Enthorpe House, however you must turn left (GR.918457) along another wide verge and ride all the way to the outskirts of Goodmanham Village.**

The ancient name Godmundingaham comes from the Celtic 'Godo' meaning an uncovered sanctuary and 'mynydiss' meaning a hilly place. The Venerable Bede thought that the great Pagan temple of Northumbria (then North of

Trail 16

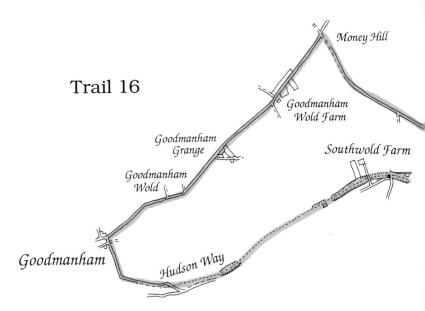

Money Hill

Goodmanham Wold Farm

Goodmanham Grange

Southwold Farm

Goodmanham Wold

Goodmanham

Hudson Way

---

the Humber) was sited at Goodmanham and in AD627 Edwin the King of Northumbria converted to Christianity at Goodmanham, burned down the Pagan Temple and went to York to be baptised on the spot where York Minster stands today. A ride around this unspoilt village is a worthwhile detour.

At the outskirts of the village your route turns left (GR.892432) and you continue riding, preferably at a walk, down the narrow lane which can be a bit slippery in places, to the old railway line which you passed under earlier on the route. Turn left onto the disused railway line. *This is known as Hudsons Way and owned by the County Council. It is a recreational Green Corridor and it is registered as a footpath but there is permissive usage for riders and pedal cyclists. Part of the line is managed as a nature sanctuary.*

Continue riding along this quiet trail for just over two miles and after crossing the fine, brick, arched bridge, you come to Kiplingcoates Station (GR.929439) which is now

known as Granny's Attic and a[n] antique shop. *Here you leave th[e] disused railway line and ride to th[e] left down the drive to come to th[e] road where you turn rig[ht] (GR.932440) and ride to th[e] crossroads (GR.941440). Here tu[rn] right and retrace your steps back t[o] Newbald Lodge .
From Newbald Lodge you have [a] choice of routes back to your parki[ng] place.

Either: take the bridleway back.
Or: use the good wide verges a[nd] follow the road which will take y[ou] back to your starting point.

* An alternative route is also availab[le] here:
If you wish you may stay on the disus[ed] railway line at Kiplingcoates Stati[on] and ride to the next excellent exit, 1.[5] miles further on at a brick wall. Y[ou] exit left then go under the brid[ge] heading south onto the bridleway nor[th] of Gardham.

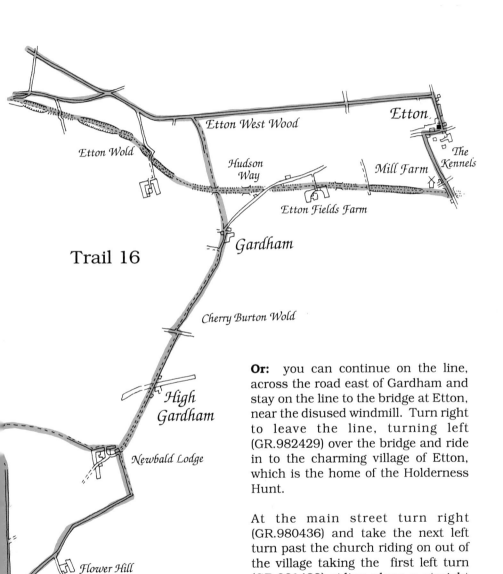

Etton West Wood

Etton

Etton Wold

The Kennels

Hudson Way

Mill Farm

Etton Fields Farm

Gardham

Trail 16

Cherry Burton Wold

High Gardham

Newbald Lodge

Flower Hill

(S)

Or: you can continue on the line, across the road east of Gardham and stay on the line to the bridge at Etton, near the disused windmill. Turn right to leave the line, turning left (GR.982429) over the bridge and ride in to the charming village of Etton, which is the home of the Holderness Hunt.

At the main street turn right (GR.980436) and take the next left turn past the church riding on out of the village taking the first left turn (GR.981439) riding along a straight road, again with good wide verges. Ride for two miles then turn left (GR.951437) to retrace your steps at Etton West Wood and so on to return to your starting point.

HOLDERNESS- HALSHAM

TRAIL 17

A 17 MILE CIRCULAR TRAIL (ANTI-CLOCKWISE)

Ordnance Survey Map:
Landranger: 107

Parking & Starting Point:
Safe, off road parking is available at Elmtree Tack Shop (GR.292277) which is the starting point of this ride. As a matter of courtesy, please telephone Mrs Travis (01964) 612391 prior to arrival.

Of Interest:
This area is known generally as Holderness and is bound on the west by Kingston Upon Hull, to the south by the River Humber and to the east by the North Sea. Although mostly flat and agricultural, there is a surprising amount of off road riding and a link from this route across Burton Carrs joins it to the Burton Pidsea ride described elsewhere in this book.

Route Description:

From your parking place, ride onto the B1362 and turn right and almost immediately turn right again down a lane towards Roos, heading due north. *This lane is visible from your starting point. You are now riding into Roos Carrs which is the low lying land surrounding the village of Roos. The village name is Friesian and means watery land and the 13th century church, surrounded by trees, is clearly visible on the edge of the village.*

Just before the village you will come to the bridge over the main drain. Turn left and go through the gate onto the bridleway, keeping the bank of the drain on your right and ride on to the edge of Fox Covert. Go through another gate and follow the drain bank for three miles.*

You will hardly see any sign of human life here unless you see a farmer at work in his fields. This main drain is called Roos Drain and is very deep and takes the water from the vast surrounding shallow bowl known as Roos Carrs and Burton Pidsea Carrs.

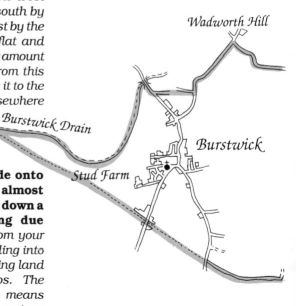

*After about 2.50 miles you will notice a farm quite close on the left and a flat tractor bridge built of sleepers to the right. This bridge is the link to the Burton Pidsea route. It may be marked on your Ordnance Survey Map as a footpath but a Public Enquiry diverted the route and upgraded it to bridleway status.

'Riders wishing to follow the Burton Pidsea trail should cross the bridge, turn right along the drain bank and follow it for 50 yards and then turn left, keeping the hedge on your left. You must now ride a straight line, at one point leaving the headland, and riding across the field you will arrive at a cross track with a hedge and headland in front of you. Turn right and follow the track to Elm Tree Farm and the metalled road which leads to Burton Pidsea village.)

If you are continuing on the main route do not cross the bridge but continue on the drain bank to meet the B1362 at a brick bridge (GR.254280)** where you turn right (GR.254280) and ride along the road for 2.50 miles to Burstwick village. *Here you will notice the beautifully restored houses on the right, of Ridgmont (which is a private residence) and Wadworth Hill which is the home and workshop of a high class cabinet maker.*

At the outskirts of the village turn right at the garage*** and ride to a T-junction where you turn right (GR.226286). Ride over the bridge and turn immediately left onto a bridleway with the large Burstwick Drain now on your left. *This bridleway has only recently been researched and claimed, it appears on the Definitive Map but may not yet appear on your Ordnance Survey Map.*

Trail 17

61

Follow the drain until you get to the old railway line. *The old railway line ran from Hull to Withernsea.* Turn left on to the railway line and ride easterly crossing the road at the old Burstwick Station which was built in 1845 and ride on to the next road crossing where there is a small parking area.

From this parking area, south of Burstwick village, ride along the old railway line for another 4 miles. *You will pass ponds used for fishing and water-skiing on the left.* At Keyingham you will leave the old railway line for a few hundred yards as part of the track through the station has been sold and it is necessary to turn left and take the leafy lane running parallel with the track to rejoin the line again after the station.

The village of Keyingham is an historic settlement inhabited by Caega and his people from whence it gets its name. As you ride towards the village, note the church on the hill. It had an elegant soaring spire used by sailors on the River Humber 2.50 miles away as a guide, but it was badly damaged in a storm and replaced with the tower in 1969.

Leaving Keyingham, ride towards Ottringham and Carr House Farm on your left. *Take care with the anti-traffic, folding barriers where the farm drive crosses the line.* **Ride directly through Ottringham Station and into a green tunnel of vegetation which will take even a very big horse!

When you come to a fallen log and a farm crossing, leave the railway line and take the first track on the left (GR.282251). Ride past the end of the wood staying on the track and negotiate several 90 degree turns until you arrive at a green gate at Churchlands Farm.

Go through the gate and on up the main farm drive to meet a road (GR.296260). Turn left and then take the next left turning which will bring you back to your parking place.

NOTES:
There are two opportunities to make your ride shorter should you so wish.

**At the brick bridge turn left and ride along the road to Halsham village. On the left you will notice the Mausoleum of the Constable family. Work commenced on the building in 1790 and took ten years*

Halsham

to complete. Family members are still interred there and opposite is a very old brick building which was a free school and alms hospital founded by the Constable family in 1579. It is now a private residence called Halsham House. Behind and to the west of it is All Saints Church, Halsham, built in the 12th century and restored in the 19th century.

At the Halsham Arms public house, turn right and ride in a southerly direction towards Ottringham. When you get to the railway at Ottringham station, turn left and rejoin the main route at **

***Turn left at the garage and when you reach a T-junction, turn left and ride into the village of Burstwick. There used to be a castle here given by William the Conqueror to the Earls of Albemarle. In 1306 Edward I imprisoned the Queen of Robert the Bruce for one year, but there is little or no visible evidence of the castle now. Ride on through the village passing two public houses and out into open country. In a short distance you will come to the old railway line. Turn left along here and rejoin the route at ***

The Northern Shire Horse Centre, North Newbold (see trail 16)

A 8 MILE CIRCULAR TRAIL (CLOCKWISE)

Ordnance Survey Map:

Landranger: 106

Parking & Starting Point:

Parking is available by prior arrangement with Mrs Abu Hamdan at High Belthorpe Livery, Bishop Wilton (GR.781542), telephone 01759 368238. There will be a small fee charged for parking.

Of Interest:

This ride is on the edge of the Vale of York with lovely views up onto the Wolds. It tours around the charming scenic village of Bishop Wilton. High Belthorpe House is itself of some antiquity and remains of the moat are clearly visible.

Route Description:

Leave your parking place and turn right on to the bridleway which takes you across two small chalk streams to the village of Fangfoss. When you meet the road (GR.765532), turn right and ride for about two miles heading north west, passing a right turn for the village of Gowthorpe. *Note the old wartime bomber airfield to the left which is now a small rural industrial estate. Also to the left you will see the high security fencing of HM Prison at Full Sutton.* **At a slight right/left dog leg in the road, where there is a farm to the left, turn right (GR.751551) and go**

through a gate onto a bridleway.

Ride to the end of the first field an then following the track go left right and straight ahead throug the second field to come to a gate i the hedge. Go through the gate an turn left following the headland which is waymarked, until you ge to a grass and stone road - part o Minster Way.

Follow this bridleway through t the tarmac road north of Youlthorp (GR.765559). Turn right. Keep lef in the village and follow the roa signs along the lane all the way t the outskirts of Bishop Wilton. A you approach the village, take th first turn right (GR.789553) an after 0.25 miles you will see a hedge land to the left (GR.792549). Tur here and ride along this lane. *Not the small old fashioned cottage field and gardens.*

At the tarmac village street tur left and then almost immediatel turn right. The church will be t your right. After the church, tur right and then turn right again t ride parallel with the stream.

Narrow roads criss-cross the green an stream which are the heart of th lovely village. The beautiful church St Edith was restored in the 19t century and has a fine carved ston Norman Arch in the porch. The churc floor is a copy of a mosaic floor in th Vatican.

Ride along the street to 'The Fleece' Public House.

Notice the interesting village noticeboard on the green opposite. It is worthwhile riding along the street and back to admire the different styles of rural architecture.

From 'The Fleece', turn left (GR.797551) and take the next turn on the right (GR.798549). This is a lane which becomes a bridleway and runs beside Bishop Wilton Beck. Take the next turn right (GR.794546) and then at the road, turn left, 300 yards ahead you will see the drive that will take you back to your starting point.

Trail 18

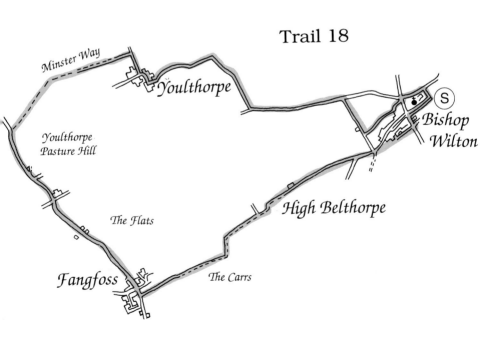

BARTON-UPON-HUMBER

**A 15 MILE CIRCULAR TRAIL
(ANTI-CLOCKWISE)**

Ordnance Survey Map:
Landranger: 112

Parking & Starting Point:
Parking is available in the wide main street of Wootton village or on the verges just to the west of Wootton (GR.082160). Your route is described from the main street in Wootton.

Route Description:

Leave your parking place riding in a westerly direction and ride along the wide grassy verges for almost a mile until you come to a crossroads (GR.062151). Turn right and ride along the wide verges to Burnham. At the village crossroads, go straight across and follow the village road northwards, towards Barton-upon-Humber. Ride for a little over a mile and then go straight across at the crossroads. Look for and take a bridleway on a farm drive to the left (GR.049190), in the dip of the road. Ride towards the old farm buildings and then go right up the headland.

Keeping the hedge to your right, follow this track and the waymarked bridleway which will take you along track, headland and more track, going through two gates, one of which is next to a cattle grid and on to meet the B1218 (GR.026197) which is a tarmac road. Turn right along the road and after a mile, turn left (GR.031212) into a lane which has houses to your right and open fields to the left.

Ride straight on over the A15. Here there are super views of the Humber Bridge to your right. *This is the longest single span suspension bridge in the world.*

At a left-hand bend in the road, take the bridleway on the left (GR.008200) and follow this wide grassy, well used route south easterly for 2 miles, to the B1218. Turn right. *Take care here as the view is not clear from the end of the bridleway.* **Ride along the left-hand verge with the flow of traffic and take the next turn left to go back over the A15. (GR.028170).**

Because of a new slip-road, the route now described varies from that on the Ordnance Survey Map.

Turn right down the slip-road and turn left down the bridleway which is half-way down. Go through the gate and ride along the side of the fence. You are now on the Viking Way and for the next 4 miles there is good going. Cross straight over the first road, but keep an eye out for traffic coming from under the bridge on the right. At the second road ride straight ahead for about 200 yards then turn back onto the bridleway (GR.051148). At the third road where there are bushes and trees turn left (GR.064136) and ride to the crossroads (GR.062150). Turn right and so ride on to return to your starting point.

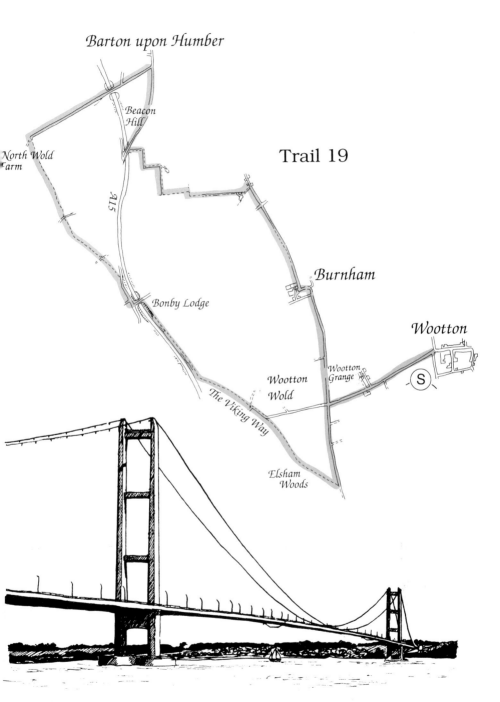

Barton upon Humber

Beacon Hill

North Wold Farm

Trail 19

A15

Burnham

Wootton

Bonby Lodge

Wootton Grange

Wootton Wold

The Viking Way

S

Elsham Woods

Humber Bridge

67

A 15 MILE TRAIL

Ordnance Survey Map:
Landranger: 112

Parking & Starting Point:
Parking is available in the wide main street in Wootton village or on the verges just to the west of the village (GR.082160).

Of Interest:
This ride takes place on lovely rolling, wide grass verges and sections of The Viking Way.

Route Description:

From your parking place, ride north on the wide verges along the minor road. At the first crossroads turn left (GR.078175) and ride to Burnham village. Take the first turn left (GR.059171) and ride along the very wide verges towards Melton Ross. Cross straight over the first cross roads and ride straight ahead. You will pass a gas installation on the left, a bridleway crosses the road and then the road goes downhill in trees. Your route turns right (GR.066133) along a well defined track and this arcs left for a little over a mile. At the tarmac junction, turn left (GR.054118). Follow this lane as it leads under the A180 to Melton Ross.

At the T-junction, (GR.070108) turn left and ride back on the road bridge over the A180. At the end of the tree planting you passed on your outward journey, turn left onto the bridleway (GR.065136) and follow the well defined Viking Way for a little over one mile. When you come to the road, keep left and at the next road junction leave the tarmac and follow the bridleway which is straight ahead. At the next road junction, which is in a dip with a bridge to the left, turn right (GR.037159) and ride along the road to Burnham village. At the crossroads turn right and at the next crossroads, turn left and ride back to your parking place.

68

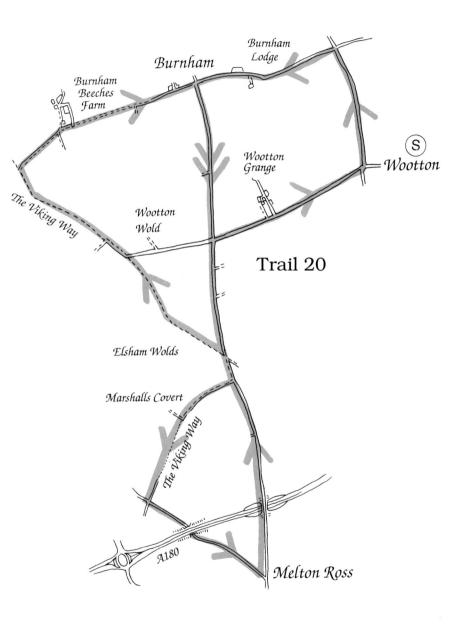

Burnham Lodge

Burnham

Burnham Beeches Farm

The Viking Way

Wootton Grange

Wootton Wold

ⓢ Wootton

Trail 20

Elsham Wolds

Marshalls Covert

The Viking Way

A180

Melton Ross

A 15 MILE CIRCULAR TRAIL (ANTI-CLOCKWISE)

Ordnance Survey Maps:
Landranger: 112 & 113

Parking & Starting Point:
Parking is available on a green lane, south-east of Barnetby village (GR.078089). Please keep to the sides of the lane as farm vehicles have access along the lane. Your ride is described from here.

Route Description:

From your parking place ride south-east along the green lane. As it dips downhill take the lesser track going right and then turn right (GR.084080) and follow this well defined farm road and bridleway all the way to the tarmac road just north of Bigby village. Take great care exiting onto the road as it is a steep downhill exit.

Turn left (GR.059076) along the road and ride through the village to a T-junction. Turn right, then left along a minor lane and ride for 0.25 miles. Turn sharp left uphill towards the trees, passing a church on the right. At the main road (GR.067065), cross directly over and ride along the lovely verges over Somerby Top.

After the farm, the track becomes clay and then it goes into a cultivated field. The bridleway, not always delineated, goes straight ahead across the field. At the headland, veer right and continu to the end of the field where yo come to a green lane. Turn righ (GR.090078). Take the next trac going right (GR.092076) and rid over Searby Top to the road. At th main road, turn left, then right int Searby village. Continue going righ through the village and the roa bears left (GR.071056).

Bigby

Somerby

Hall

Ride for 0.75 miles to a T-junction. Turn left and ride up the hill. At the main road, turn left and take the lane on the right (GR.081054), using the good verges. Ride straight ahead for almost two miles to the wood. Follow the track right which skirts the woods, until you come to a tarmac road. Turn left and at the crossroads, turn left again. Follow the road for a little over a mile and just after the woods, turn left (GR.1014084) onto a well waymarked bridleway which skirts the woods.

To your right you will see Humberside Airport. The bridleway passes very close to the landing lights at the end of the runway. Watch and listen for aircraft!!

Continue along the track which passes through two sets of large metal gates, then through Barnetby Wold Farm before bringing you back to your starting point.

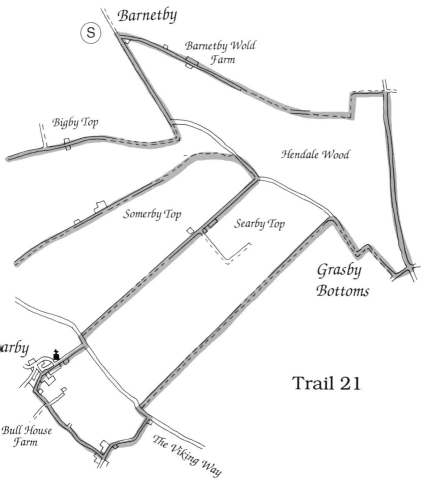

Trail 21

71

AN 18 MILE CIRCULAR TRAIL (ANTI-CLOCKWISE)

Ordnance Survey Map:
Landranger: 106

Parking & Starting Point:
Parking is available by prior arrangement with Mr & Mrs Winlow at Seaton Old Hall Farm, Seaton Ross, telephone: 01759   318469. (GR.779396).   A small fee will be charged.   This is also your starting point.

Of Interest:
This is a flat, rural ride on quiet lanes, bridleways and old railway line, passing through the quiet scenic villages of Everingham and Seaton Ross.

Route Directions:

Ride down the farm drive to the road and turn left (GR.774398). Follow this road to the A163 (GR.768379), turn left and ride for about 200 yards to a right-hand bend where you turn left (GR.770380) onto the old railway line which lies through the big timber fence.   The railway line take you across the north side of Holme-on-Spalding Moor village.

Continue to follow the line through two old railway stations and on to the A163 (GR.840405).   Turn left and ride a very short distance along the wide verge to take the headland bridleway to your left, keeping the hedge on your left. Follow the track heading north, through to Brouncey

Farm.   Here there is a staggered crossroads of bridleways, so ride slightly left, then right and along the headland with the hedge on your left. Follow the waymarkers which make a left and right turn and then meander on until you come to the tarmac lane* (GR.828432). Turn left and ride to the estate village of Everingham.

Seaton Ross

Seaton Old Hall

(S)

Water End

*Here you may choose an alternative to lengthen your route if you wish: Turn left (GR.814429), ride for about one mile and then take a clearly defined bridleway on the left and follow the waymarkers through to Park Farm. Turn down the farm drive, also a bridleway, and ride to the road. Turn right (GR.822412) and follow the road round the park to your right and rejoin the route in Everingham.

At the T-junction turn right (GR.803426) and ride for 2.50 miles on the twisting lane following the road signs to Seaton Ross.

In Seaton Ross you can see the 12 ft diameter sundial on one of the cottages. Seaton Ross has been placed several times in the 'Britain in Bloom' competition and the flowers are especially pretty early in the spring and for the annual agricultural show held each year on the first weekend in July.

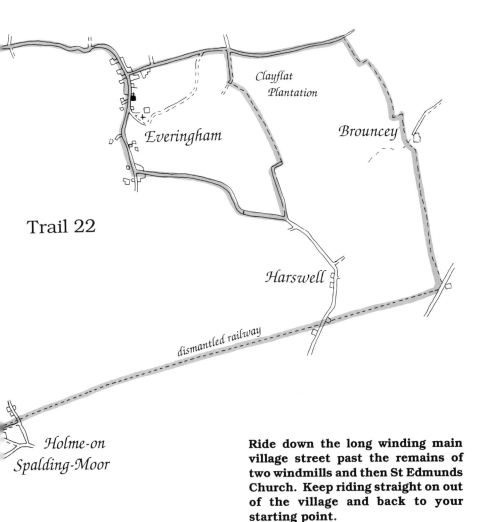

Trail 22

Clayflat Plantation

Everingham

Brouncey

Harswell

dismantled railway

Holme-on Spalding-Moor

Ride down the long winding main village street past the remains of two windmills and then St Edmunds Church. Keep riding straight on out of the village and back to your starting point.

NEWPORT

A 11 MILE CIRCULAR TRAIL (ANTI-CLOCKWISE)

Ordnance Survey Map:
Landranger: 106

Parking & Starting Point:
Parking is available at East Yorkshire Equestrian Centre, Stoney Carr Lane, Newport (GR.865318) by prior arrangement with Mrs Elliott - telephone 01430 440835. A small fee will be charged for parking.

Of Interest:
This ride is entirely flat and takes place mostly on sandy tracks and very quiet lanes.

Route Description:

From your parking place, leave the Equestrian Centre and turn left along the lane. Follow the lane all the way to South Carr Farm, ignoring other bridleway markers en route. At South Carr Farm (GR.861329), keep slightly right, following the waymarkers through the farm and out through a gate at the back of the farm. You are now on the 'back road' to South Carr Farm. Turn right and follow the track which will take you to the next farm - North Carr Farm (GR.866338).

Follow the waymarkers until you meet the road where you turn left. After a short distance, the track forks and you take the right fork leading towards a small planting of

trees. Continue on the track going through the trees. As you leave the trees, there is a dyke on the left. Turn left here (GR.860344), keeping the dyke on your right. *Along this sandy track you may just see sand lizards or snakes basking in the sun on a hot day, but usually the beat of the horses hooves frightens them off. This is also an interesting area for bird watchers.*

Stay on this track for about one mile following the line of the drain. *You will see Wholsea Grange Farm across the field to your right.* **Cross the dyke on your right and ride to Wholsea Grange Farm. Follow the waymarkers through the farm yard going right and then left (GR.848346), and leave by riding down the main farm drive (GR.845345).**

At the end of the drive you will meet the road. *On the left is a parking area and the old Market Weighton Canal Lockpit, known as 'Sodhouse Lock'. There is a bridleway marker to the left showing a route alongside the canal. This route is a dead-end but makes a pleasant out and back ride. The canal to the right has actually been filled in having been 'cleaned out' by Italian prisoners during the Second World War.*

From the end of Wholsea Grange Farm drive, ride straight ahead to the T-junction where you turn left along the lane. The lane is narrow but is usually very quiet, it bears

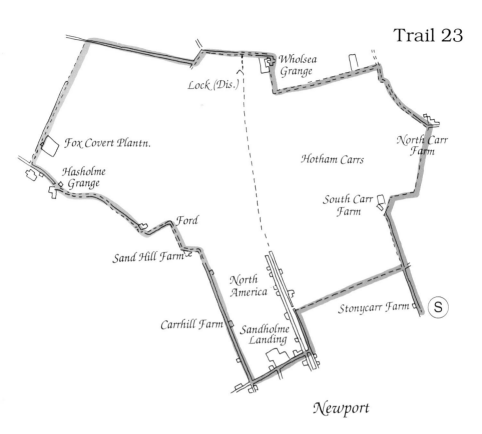

Newport

right and then goes straight on for 0.50 miles. Look for and follow the bridleway marker to the left which leads you along the flat headlands, across a small timber bridge to go right along more headlands, exiting onto the road opposite Hasholme Hall (GR.821332).

Turn left here and follow this quiet lane, ignoring any side turnings. Ride past newly planted trees. At the point marked 'Ford' (GR.837326) there is a substantial bridge. Cross the bridge and ride along the lane to a T-junction. At the T-junction (GR.846309), turn left and ride past the greenhouses and along the road until you come to the Market Weighton Canal. Cross the bridge

to the Canal Bank East and turn left (GR.853313). Ride to the Pumping Station (GR.851317), which is quite obvious and turn right down a well defined bridleway to Stoney Carr Lane. At the lane, turn right and so return to your starting point.

LEVEN

**A 20 MILE CIRCULAR TRAIL
(ANTI-CLOCKWISE)**

Ordnance Survey Map:
Landranger: 107

Parking & Starting Point:
A small fee will be charged for private parking near the start of the ride. This can be arranged by telephoning 01964 533739 prior to arrival. The starting point for the ride is Bewholme village (GR.165500).

Of Interest:
Much of this ride is on quiet country lanes, but the rural scenery is attractive, if flat. The start is at Bewholme village. 'Begum' the old name for Bewholme, means 'at the bends of the stream', although there is little visible of this now.

Route Description:

Your ride starts in Bewholme village. From the south, take the first road going left by the school and ride for two miles along the lane. Take the next left turn (GR.140489) and ride past the houses and the end of the old airfield runway to take the bridleway to your right (GR.143479). *This is due to be slightly diverted so may not appear on the ground quite as it does on the Ordnance Survey maps, but follow the waymarkers through to Brandesburton.*

Cross directly over the A165 just

north of the roundabout and continue past the Norman church. On the main village street, turn right, ride round the bend and then turn right again. Take the next turn right, with the grounds of the hospital now on your left. *This is Brandesburton Mental Hospital, formerly Brandesburton Hall and was built in 1772. At a later date it was lived in by a big game hunter called Colonel Harrison who brought home some Pygmies to live at the Hall. They used to use nail clenchings to tip their arrows to shoot rabbits in the grounds!*

At the end of the Hall grounds, turn left (GR.117480) and ride along a bridleway following the waymarkers westward to the road north of Burshill (GR.098485). At the road, turn left and then take the first turn right, continue through the village and take the next left turn (GR.090478), signposted Leven. *Along this delightful lane you will cross two small streams and the dovecote-topped Heighholme Coach House.*

After 1.50 miles you will come to a T-junction (GR.095454) where you turn left and ride straight to the village of Leven. *The Ordnance Survey map shows the A165 running through Leven, but since the opening of the by-pass in May 1994, the village is much quieter.* **At the main street, turn right and ride past the pub and garage and shortly after, turn left (GR.110444) onto a bridleway.** *This has recently*

Trail 24

been the subject of a major diversion order due to the building of the by-pass.

you now ride TO the by-pass, turn right and ride one mile along a fenced track and round the roundabout, using specially constructed 'holding pens'. This ensures you cross these busy roads where the traffic is moving at its lowest. Ride all the way round the roundabout and then along the other side of the by-pass, again in a fenced track, until the track turns sharp right away from the road and you pass between fields to the lane south of Catwick.

turn left (GR.128449), ride to the village Hall, turn right and follow the road past the church. *Note the concrete 'patch' in the tree in the churchyard, put there many years ago to stop the rain getting in and rotting the trunk.*

At the next T-junction (GR.133454), turn right and ride away from the village past Cobble Hall. *Cobble Hall is built as it says, of sea cobbles, and is visible from the road. It is now painted white.*

After about 1.25 miles you will come to a planting of fairly young trees, turn left here and after a stream take the next left turn. Ride for about one mile and cross directly over the B1244 and continue until you get back to the end of the airfield bridleway from where you retrace your steps back to the start.

BUBWITH TO LONDESBOROUGH

A 15 MILE LINEAR ROUTE (WEST TO EAST)

Ordnance Survey Map:
Landranger: 106

Parking & Starting point:
Parking is available at Thornes Motor Services, Derwent Garage, Bubwith. Telephone: 01757 288378 but **ONLY** by prior arrangement. A small fee will be charged and parking will be dependent on the coach traffic at the garage. (GR.710364). This is also the starting point for your ride.

NB. Remember that this is a linear trail so do not forget to make arrangements for someone to meet you at the other end to bring you home after your ride.

Of Interest:
This route is mostly flat and uses the Bubwith Rail Trail and rural bridleways, then quiet lanes to end at the picnic area at Towthorpe Corner, east of Shiptonthorpe. Bubwith is a very ancient village dating back to Viking times. Until the barrage was built down-river at Barmby on the Marsh, the River Derwent was tidal past Bubwith and during winter floods the low lying area around often became wildlife sanctuaries for migrating birds.

In the village, note the 12th Century church built from stone brought to the area via the river. In the churchyard is a memorial to the men of 78th Squadron who were based at nearby Breighton Airfield during the Second World War. One of the 'old trades' of Bubwith was the growing of teasels which were used to 'tease' or comb wool in the West Riding Woollen Mills. The village is also the home of a Residential Theatre and Television School where students from around the world go to study and perform plays.

Route Description:

Leave the garage and turn left along the village street on the A163. *Traffic is not usually either fast or dense.* **Take the right turn towards Gunby and Breighton. After 0.50 miles you will come to the old railway line.** *To the right is 'Dingle Dell', part of the old line but now a nature reserve and woodland area unfortunately there is no access for riders, cyclists or wheelchairs - only walkers!*

Allber

Harlthorpe   *Foggathorpe*

Highfield

(S) *Bubwith*

Turn left (GR.713357). *The Rail Trail is on the definitive map as a footpath but there is permissive use for riding and cycling.*

Ride along the old line crossing two roads and at the third road, A163, you cross diagonally to the right - take care and listen for traffic. Continue again on the rail trail which now takes you across the north side of Holme on Spalding Moor and crosses over a small stream, past the Dale Farm Foods Factory on the right and then on over the mown grass of the Old Station House.

You will see the highest ground in the area 'Church Hill' with All Saints Church standing on it. This is mentioned in the Domesday Book 1086.

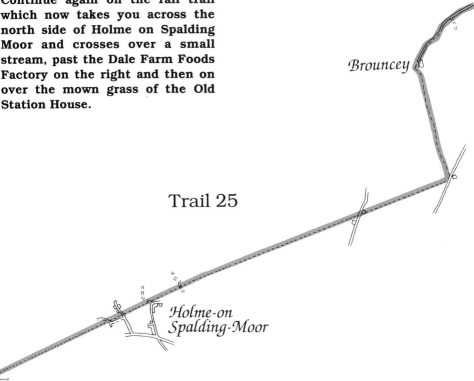

Trail 25

Brouncey

Holme-on
Spalding-Moor

A note of interest: In this village, Professor Norman Feather, son of a past headmaster of the village school, was one of seven people who first split the atom, and a school friend of Professor Feather was Sir Aubrey Burke who worked on the engineering and construction of the R100 Airship which crossed the Atlantic in 1930 and was built south-west of here at Spaldington, near Howden.

Continue along the Rail Trail and pass through Harswell Station, crossing another minor road. You now come to the end of the Rail Trail and are at the A163 (GR.840406) again.   Turn left heading north, and ride along the wide verge for about 25 yards and then turn left along a headland bridleway with a hedge on your left.

Follow this to Brouncey Farm and past the buildings. Turn right along the farm drive, which is still bridleway, and ride 1.50 miles to Shiptonthorpe. You are now at the A1079 trunk road (GR.851433) which can be very busy so cross with care. Go directly over this road and follow the quiet lane towards Londesborough for about 2.50 miles. Take the first road right (GR.865453), or detour into this charming village.

From the right turn, you ride along the lane which skirts the estate on your left, to the roundabout which is the A163 again! Turn left on the grass verge and ride to the picnic area in the lay-by next to the Garage - this is visible from the roundabout, where your transport should await you.

Trail 25 Cont.

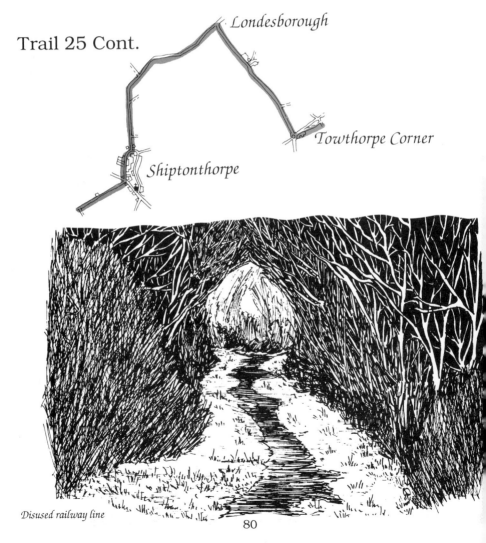

Disused railway line

Robeanne House Farm
Bed & Breakfast and Stables

Open all year. large purpose built stables
All weather menage - individual
turn out paddocks
Safe Parking
Farrier for emergencies.
Good hunting country (Middleton &
Holderness) also Hunsley Beagles

A friendly welcome for your friends,
relatives and business colleagues
Dogs and Horses by arrangement

ROBEANNE HOUSE FARM
Driffield Lane
Shiptonthorpe
York YO4 3LB
Tel: (01430) 873312

MEMBER
Yorkshire and
Humberside
Tourist Board

English Tourist Board
Listed

RIDE WITH:

CARE

- For the Land

COURTESY

- To other users

CONSIDERATION

- For the Farmer

LOOKING FOR SOMEWHERE DIFFERENT FOR YOU AND YOUR HORSE TO STAY

Then Try

Aughton Hall
Aughton, York. YO4 4PG

A delightful Manorial Country House set in 16 acres of historically important grounds in the
heart of the Lower Derwent Valley Nature Reserve and yet only 13 miles from
the historic City of York.

Peace and tranquillity awaits you in this Country lover's Paradise

Large Comfortable Lounge with log fire in winter • Separate TV Lounge for non smokers • Licensed

Lovely moated grounds overlooking open countryside

Delightful En-suite Bedrooms each with colour TV, Radio/Alarm Clock,
Refreshment Tray, Trouser Press

HORSES CAN GRAZE OR BE STABLED

For illustrated Bed and Breakfast details please telephone
01757 289046

The village of Aughton is located about 8 miles North of Junction 37 of the M62 motorway

LONDESBOROUGH TO TICKTON

TRAIL 26

A 15 MILE LINEAR ROUTE (WEST TO EAST)

Ordnance Survey Map:
Landranger: 106 & 107

Parking & Starting Point:
Parking is available in the Towthorpe Picnic Area at Londesborough (GR.879440) and your ride is described from here.

NB. Remember that this is a linear trail so do not forget to make arrangements for someone to meet you at the other end to bring you home after your ride.

Of Interest:
This ride follows on from the Bubwith to Londesborough linear ride and is bisected by several other circular rides. It follows 'Hudsons Way' a County Council recreational route shown on the definitive map as a footpath but with permissive use for riders and cyclists, moving on to quiet country lanes and a grassy bridleway.

Route Description:

From the picnic area, the bridleway is indicated going south and also marked 'Wolds Way'. It takes you to Goodmanham village. Follow the bridleway to the village and turn left at the church. Take the first right turning (GR.892432) which is down a narrow lane - take care, it is a bit slippery in places. When you reach the old railway line, turn left and ride along 'Hudson's Way'. *This area is known as Spring Wells where numerous springs surface where the porous chalk above meets the impervious clay underneath. There is a 40ft deep borehole here which supplies 0.1 million gallons of water per day to Market Weighton Reservoir.*

The section of line you are now riding on is managed as a nature reserve and compliments another nature reserve in an adjacent quarry which you pass on the left. This is a Site of Special Scientific Interest (SSSI), because of the plants growing there. There is no entry on horseback, but you can tie up and visit on foot.

Continue along the trail, crossing a large brick bridge. *This bridge was built during the reign of Queen Victoria and is a most unusual style, being without keystones.* **The next port of call is 'Granny's Attic' at the old Kiplingcoates Station.** *Granny's Attic sells antiques. You will also find a tea room, car park and picnic area here.*

Leave the old station still on the old railway line. *As you do so, you will note an old quarry on the right. During the construction of the rail track in 1865, a burial ground was found here which contained 50 skeletons and domestic articles which had been buried with the bodies.*

You will now go across a farm lane and into a long cutting with a slight uphill gradient. *Imagine the steam train of times gone by puffing up this hill towards Beverley.* **In a short distance you cross the new Gardham bridleway entry/exit ramp where other rides bisect this route. Ignore this bridleway and continue on the rail trail across the Gardham/Etton road and 1.50 miles later, at a large brick bridge, exit right and up to the road.**

To your left you can see an old windmill. **Turn left over the bridge and turn down the next lane on your right (GR.982429). At the B1248 (GR.992430), cross straight over and follow the excellent verges to the T-junction. Turn left and follow this lane to the outskirts of Leconfield village.**

The name Leconfield derives from Llecen-Fylliad meaning a flat stone in a gloomy shade. Leconfield was a sacred Druid site, but today it is a bright and busy village.

In 1541 Henry VIII visited the now dismantled Leconfield Castle, home of the Percy family of Northumberland.

Ride on until you come to a T-junction (GR.010439) where you turn right down a street of more modern houses and bungalows. Follow this road until you reach the A164. *Here the traffic may be busy, so cross the road with care.* **Turn right and use the cycle lane for 200 yards and then turn left, signposted Arram.**

Trail 26

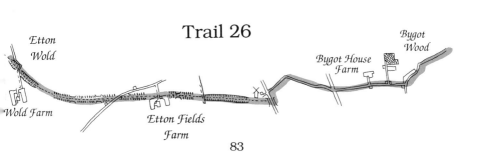

Etton Wold

Bygot Wood

Bygot House Farm

Wold Farm

Etton Fields Farm

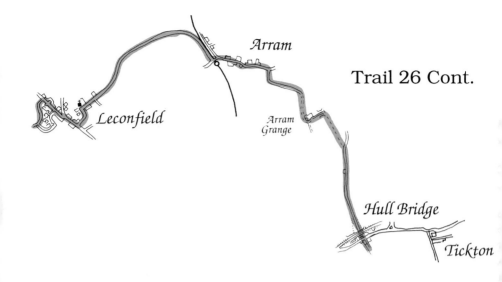

Arram

Leconfield

Arram Grange

Hull Bridge

Tickton

Continue riding along this road and out of the village, passing St Catherine's Church, which was founded in the 7th Century. You will now come onto a lane with a tarmac surface, concrete edges, flat verges and well kept hedges which prescribes a 180 degree arc to the right over one mile around the perimeter of the old RAF station built in the mid-1930's. *The airfield first saw service in 1937 with Heyford Bi-planes, followed by wartime Spitfires and Hurricanes, then Halifax and Blenheim Bombers. After the war came Hunters and Javelins followed by Lightenings. Today the air is altogether more peaceful as the base is home of the Army School of Mechanical Transport.*

At Arram station, go directly across the railway lines and continue into Arram village. As the road peters out at the end of the village (GR.043441), turn right and follow the bridleway to Arram Grange. Just past the farm turn left and ride on over an old brick bridge which crosses Barmston Drain. Turn immediately right (GR.051435) with the drain on your right and ride the 1.50 miles to Tickton. Go through the gate, under the A1035 flyover to end your ride at Tickton village (GR.055417).

**A 15 MILE CIRCULAR TRAIL
(ANTI-CLOCKWISE)**

Ordnance Survey Map:
Landranger: 106

Parking & Starting Point:
Parking is available at the East Riding
Equestrian Centre, Stoney Carr Lane,
Newport (GR.865318) by prior
arrangement with Mrs Elliott. Please
telephone 01430 440835. A small
charge will be made for parking.

Of Interest:
*This ride is mostly on roads with good
wide verges and bridleways, but it
does include rides around the very
attractive little villages of North Cave,
Everthorpe and Hotham.*

Route Description:

**Leave the Equestrian Centre and
turn right. Ride along the road in
the direction of the M62. About
half-way up the motorway fly-over
bridge, turn left and ride along a
concrete road past 'Gate House' to
turn left along the clay track which
runs parallel with the road.
Continue to ride all the way to the
end of the slip road (B1230) towards
North Cave.**

**Leaving the interchange behind,
turn down the first lane on the right
(GR.878316). This is Common Lane
West and is just before the Garden
Centre. Ride again to the edge of
the expressway, now the A63, and**
turn left along the wide green lane.
*Compare as you ride, the old form of
transport with the new.* **Ride straight
ahead for about one mile.** *Please do
not attempt to use the bridleway which
you pass to the right as there is no
bridge across the dual carriageway
and there is no alternative way to get
across.*

**After about one mile, you will cross
the beck (GR.892314) and ride
straight ahead to the road. Turn
right and then turn left (GR.899316)
to continue to Everthorpe village.**
This is a quiet, unspoilt, rural village.
**Ride until you come to the end of
the houses and then turn left
(GR.910320) to double back on the
'other' village road. You will then
cross the bridge over the old Hull
and Barnsley Railway line. Continue
to the T-junction (GR.900323) at
North Cave.**

*The station at North Cave was built in
1885. The last train passed through in
1957 and the line was closed in 1964.
The last passenger train in the early
1950's was pulled by the locomotive
'Sir William Henton Carver'. This is
significant as Sir William Henton Carver
lived at 'The Croft' which is amongst
the trees, directly opposite the T-
junction. Sir William was also on board
the train for this historic journey.*

*Although this is such a small village,
North Cave has a wealth of both
fascinating and historic interest. If you
ride to the North Cave Church, it is*

possible to purchase a booklet called 'Walking around North Cave'. A most interesting guide.

To get to the church, turn right at the T-junction, then go straight ahead at the War Memorial. Turn right at the shop and ride along Church Street to the Church. The Vicarage is opposite in the trees, next to the playing fields.

You can ride most parts of the 'Walking Route', except Paper Mill, Upper Mill, Fish Ponds and Quaker Well. However, if you look at the map in the centre of the booklet you can clearly plot your own course around these bits.

Having visited the village, return to the Church and leave on the B1230 going past Manor Farm. Ride for 1.50 miles to meet the A1034 (GR.916337). This road is very busy but it does have a good verge. Turn left and ride for a few hundred yards before turning left again (GR.914341) onto a minor road with very wide verges. Continue along here to Hotham village.

The name Hotham, is Anglo Saxon and means sheltered hamlet. In 1066 100 people lived in this prospering village but by 1251 it is described as having the same population but 15 ruinous cottages. Could this have been an early form of recession? The village is mainly based on agriculture and has a pleasant public house.

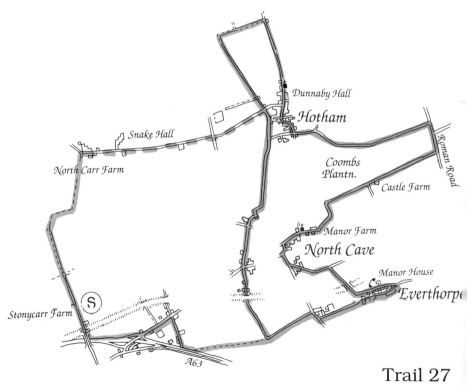

Trail 27

In the village itself, at the gates to Hotham Hall, turn right and ride past the pub to the church. Continue straight ahead onto a track (GR.894346). After 0.75 miles, take the bridleway track to the left (GR.892355) and ride for 0.50 miles. Turn left (GR.892343) and ride back to the village road.*

Ride straight ahead along this rural lane back to North Cave. When you meet the first crossroads, ride straight ahead with the beck appearing to your left. At the B1230 go straight across with care, keeping to the beck bank. *You will now ride under the Hull and Barnsley Railway.* Stay by the side of the beck until you get to the bridleway junction (GR.892314) which you passed on the outward journey. Turn right and retrace your steps back to your parking place.

An alternative ride back to the start is available here. To take this route, turn right and ride down the hill to the crossroads. Go directly across and down the lane passing Snake Hall to North Carr Farm. Turn left onto the bridleway and follow it through South Carr Farm and so on down the lane back to the start.

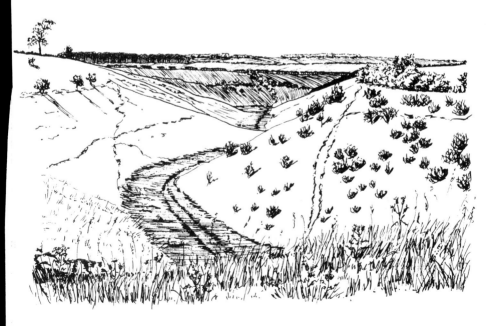

Typical Dry Dale

HIVE

A 15 MILE CIRCULAR TRAIL (CLOCKWISE)

Ordnance Survey Map:
Landranger: 106

Parking and Starting Point:
Parking is available by prior arrangement with Mrs Elliott at East Riding Equestrian Centre, Stoney Carr Lane, Newport, telephone: 01430 440835 (GR.865318). A small fee will be charged. This is also your starting point.

Route Description:

From your parking place, leave the Equestrian Centre and turn left along the lane.   After a short distance, take the waymarked bridleway to your left (GR.864322) which is a clay track, and ride to the canal.   Turn left (GR.851317) and ride to the bridge.   Cross the canal via the bridge and ride straight ahead, westwards, for 1.50 miles along quiet lanes. At the T-junction (GR.831306) by the caravans, turn right signposted Sandholme. Ride a short distance and take the next turn left (GR.829308) into the village. After passing the telephone box, bear left and then right to ride past the glasshouses which are along a lane with good verges.   Ride for about two miles to Eastrington.

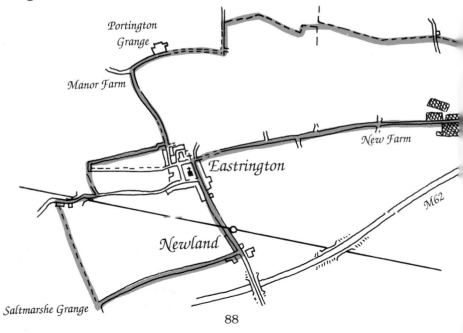

n Eastrington take the first turning eft (GR.797301) and ride until you have crossed the railway level crossing. Take the first lane on the right (GR.802293), after the level crossing, which is a waymarked bridleway, and pass Bridge Farm. This lane continues in a straight line for a little over one mile. It becomes grass and passes through a gate before arriving at Saltmarshe Grange.

Ride straight ahead through the farm and after the last cottage, turn right (GR.788288). Ride for almost one mile along a grassy bridleway with hedges. When you come to the road, turn right (GR.784298), cross the road bridge over the railway line and ride past the entrance to the picnic area, then turn left up the

At the corner of the road, turn left (GR.794303) and ride until you come to Tudor-styled timbered houses. Turn right along the waymarked bridleway which takes you up the drive of Grange Court Estate. Ride straight up the drive and go through the white gates. At the next lane, turn left (GR.800311), then right at a planting of trees, still following the waymarkers. Ride this delightful winding grass road to old farm buildings on the right. Here you track left, then right and straight ahead to a T-junction in the tracks. Turn left and then take the first turn right.

Trail 28

Stoney Carr Farm (S)

Sandholme Landing

Sandholme

M62

M62

Again you will encounter a delightful grass road. *It is interesting to compare your route now which is a rural idyll little changed over the centuries, to that you encountered at the start of your ride, so close to the motorway.*

Ride straight ahead to a lane (GR.827313) by a new house. Turn right and ride to the village. Turn left and the road bears right, signposted 'Gilberdike' Follow the signpost and take the next left turn by the caravans. Retrace your steps back to your starting point.

bridleway. At the crossroads of tracks turn right (GR.787301) and ride to the village. *You can see the church quite clearly from the crossroads of tracks.*

WITHERNWICK

AN 11 MILE CIRCULAR TRAIL
(ANTI-CLOCKWISE)

Ordnance Survey Map:
Landranger: 107

Parking & Starting Point:
Parking is available at Humberside
County Council Car Park, which is
adjacent to, but north of, The Railway
Inn at Ellerby. (GR.168394)

Of Interest:
*This is a flat, quiet ride on the back
lanes, bridleways and the old Hull to
Hornsea Railway Line. This is shown
on the definitive map as a footpath, but
with permissive use for riders and
cyclists.*

Route Description:

**Leave the car park and ride along
the railway line crossing the village
road north of The Railway Inn. The
line runs in a long cutting and then
onto an embankment, crossing the
Lambwath Stream. At the metalled
road turn right (GR.172409) and
ride along the road to the outskirts
of Withernwick village. Turn left
(GR.193407) and ride for about 0.25
miles to follow the road as it bends
right signposted 'Cowden'. Ride for
two miles along this lane and after
passing Cowden Magna Farm on the
right, and a detached house, take
the bridleway lane on the left
(GR.224418)**

Follow the waymarkers northward

and then westward to Wood Farm
*There are no waymarkers through
the farm, but the route is apparent*
**Follow the chalk road for a short
distance and then bear left onto the
bridleway to Hatfield Grange going
via Mount Pleasant Farm.** *Take care
here, there are two bridleways to
the right, both of which are better
marked than your east-west route.*

**From Hatfield Grange, ride to the
road (GR.190426). Turn right, ride
past the cemetery, and immediately
after take the bridleway on the left
(GR.188426). This leads through
Manor Farm westwards along a short
headland, through Clappisons Farm
and onto the Hull road (GR.182426)
where you should turn right and
ride to the Wrygarth Inn.**

*An alternative route from the cemetery
is to continue on the road and take the
first village road to the left which will
also take you to the Wrygarth Inn.*

**Facing Wrygarth Inn (GR.182429),
turn   left   and   ride   along
Sigglesthorne Lane until you come
to the old railway line. Turn left
onto the line, crossing one road on
the way, you will return to your
starting point.**

Wolds village cottages

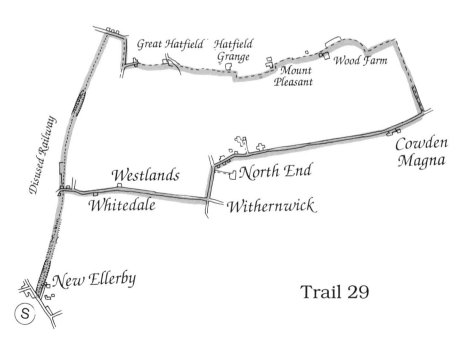

Great Hatfield

Hatfield Grange

Mount Pleasant

Wood Farm

Disused Railway

Westlands

North End

Cowden Magna

Whitedale

Withernwick

New Ellerby

(S)

Trail 29

THE BRITISH HORSE SOCIETY

The British Horse Society was founded in 1947 when two separate equestrian bodies - The National Horse Association and the Institute of the Horse and Pony Club - decided to join forces and work together for the good of both horse and rider.

It is a marriage that has proved to be a great success and the British Horse Society has steadily increased its membership from just 4000 in the late 1960's to over 60,000 in the 1990's.

By becoming members of the British Horse Society, horse lovers know they are joining a body of people with a shared interest in the horse. Members can be sure that they are contributing to the work of an equine charity with a primary aim to improve the standards of care for horses and ponies. Welfare is not only about the rescuing of horses in distress (which we do); it is also about acting to prevent abuse in the first place. There are many means to achieving this: by teaching and advising, by looking to the horse's well-being and safety, by providing off-road riding, by encouraging high standards in all equestrian establishments, and fighting for the horse's case with government and in Europe.

The British Horse Society works tirelessly towards these aims thanks to the work of its officials at Stoneleigh and its army of dedicated volunteers out in the field.

Membership benefits the horse lover as well as the horse; the Society can offer something to all equestrians, whether they are weekend riders, interested spectators or keen competitors. The benefits include free Third Party Public Liability and Personal Accident insurance, free legal advice, free publications, reductions to British Horse Society events, special facilities at the major shows, and free advice and information on any equine query.

Largely financed by its membership subscriptions, the Society welcomes the support of all horse lovers. If you are thinking of joining the Society and would like to find out more about our work, please contact the Membership Department at the following address:

The British Horse Society
British Equestrian Centre
Stoneleigh Park
Kenilworth
Warwickshire
CV8 2LR
(Telephone: 01203 696697)
Registered Charity No. 210504